Mindfulness for Therapists

Mindfulness for Therapists

Understanding Mindfulness for Professional Effectiveness and Personal Well-Being

Gerhard Zarbock, Siobhan Lynch,
Axel Ammann and Silka Ringer

WILEY Blackwell

This edition first published in English in 2015
English translation © 2015 John Wiley & Sons, Ltd.

This book is a translated version of: Gerhard Zarbock, Axel Ammann and Silka Ringer, *Achtsamkeit für Psychotherapeuten und Berater*

© 2011 Beltz Psychologie in der Verlagsgruppe

Beltz • Weinheim Basel

Registered Office
John Wiley & Sons Ltd, The Atrium, Southern Gate, Chichester, West Sussex, PO19 8SQ, UK

Editorial Offices
350 Main Street, Malden, MA 02148-5020, USA
9600 Garsington Road, Oxford, OX4 2DQ, UK
The Atrium, Southern Gate, Chichester, West Sussex, PO19 8SQ, UK

For details of our global editorial offices, for customer services, and for information about how to apply for permission to reuse the copyright material in this book please see our website at www.wiley.com/wiley-blackwell.

Library of Congress Cataloging-in-Publication Data applied for

HB ISBN: 9781118760437
PB ISBN: 9781118760420

A catalogue record for this book is available from the British Library.

Cover image: © lightstock / iStockphoto

Set in 11.5/14.5pt Palatino by SPi Publisher Services, Pondicherry, India
Printed and bound in Malaysia by Vivar Printing Sdn Bhd

1   2015

Contents

Contents

Acknowledgments

Personal Acknowledgments – Gerhard Zarbock

I would like to dedicate this book to Shodo Harada Roshi, ShoE Sabine Huskamp Zenshi and all members of the ODZ-One Drop Zen sangha. They inspire, challenge and support me as I travel on the path. I would like to thank my wife Nicole and my daughter Tara for bearing witness to the fact that I am yet to master mindfulness at home. Siobhan Lynch's work on mindfulness-based coping with university life (MBCUL) initially inspired the idea to 'do the same' for therapists. Without her dedication and mindful input, no English version of the book would have come into existence.

Personal Acknowledgments – Siobhan Lynch

I would like to thank Gerhard Zarbock for first approaching me about the project and for his continued enthusiasm for it.

I would also like to thank Esther Coalter and Joanna Boysen for their support with the initial translation of the German version. The team at Wiley have been enthusiastic throughout the process and I would like to thank Darren Reed, Karen Shield and Olivia Wells in particular. I am fortunate to be part of the Breathworks community and the Mindfulness for Students Network, both of which are sources of inspiration. I am thankful for the kindness and encouragement shown to me by Katharine Rimes, Elena Antonova, Ben Baig and Nicola Fear. I would like to thank my PhD supervisor, Harlad Walach, and my friends Majella Horan and Margo Campbell for their words of wisdom. I am forever grateful for Andreas Sommer's ongoing support and (brutally) honest feedback ☺. Finally, I would like to thank my mother, Ann Taylor, for her many hours of proofreading, which she did with good humour (often at short notice and at inconvenient times).

Personal Acknowledgments – Axel Ammann

I would like to thank all the countless great people who inspired me on my path, especially HoKai Österle, Norbert RinDo Hämmerle, Paul Stammeier and Stephen Kinryu-Jien Hayes. Special thanks go to my wife Tatjana – moon of my life – and my son Aaron – my sun and stars ☺.

Personal Acknowledgments – Silka Ringer

I would like to thank Dr. Angela Roth-Isigkeit for sparking my curiosity about yoga by talking about her own experiences and Dipl.-Psych. Petra Luck for being my first yoga teacher. Her early teaching helped me see the benefits of yoga for myself, especially how it could help both calm and energise. Since then I have continued to benefit from her weekly yoga classes. In my first intensive yoga training I discovered the versatility of yoga thanks to the integrated approach of Yoga Vidya e. V. and the yoga teachers who worked there. In terms of the relationship between my therapeutic work and mindfulness, I gained a great deal from attending seminars by Mrs Dipl.-Psych. Bettina Lohmann. I also benefited greatly from working together with Dr Alexandra Gall-Peters – we worked together in Skillsgroups with the mindfulness approach taught by Dialectical Behavior Therapy (DBT). There were and are, of course, many informal discussions with mindfulness practitioners – not least with the participants of our courses – which have been at least as influential both for me and for my contributions to this book as reading relevant literature. I would also like to thank Dr Antje Burfeind and Dr Susan Erler, who supported the development of the German version of this book by patient proofreading and thoughtful suggestions.

Image Credits

Illustrations: Claudia Styrsky, Munich

Photographs at the beginning of chapters: Gerhard Zarbock, Hamburg

Photographs in Chapter 3: Annika Sommerfeldt, Heiligenhafen; Axel Ammann, Hamburg

1

Welcome

Before we begin you might like to pause for a moment and consider what 'mindfulness' means to you. What thoughts or images pop up? Perhaps you already know about mindfulness and have your own personal practice? Or maybe this is all quite new for you?

There is no single 'right' answer or absolute definition of mindfulness, not least because the term is used in many different ways in the literature (Hayes & Wilson, 2003). However, perhaps the most useful starting point is the ever-popular definition given by Jon Kabat-Zinn, who developed mindfulness-based stress reduction (MBSR) with colleagues back in the late 1970s. Kabat-Zinn describes mindfulness as: "paying attention in a particular way, on

Mindfulness for Therapists: Understanding Mindfulness for Professional Effectiveness and Personal Well-Being, First Edition. Gerhard Zarbock, Siobhan Lynch, Axel Ammann and Silka Ringer.
© 2015 John Wiley & Sons, Ltd. Published 2015 by John Wiley & Sons, Ltd.
Companion Website: www.wiley.com/go/zarbock/mindfulnessfortherapists

purpose, in the present moment, and non-judgmentally" (1994, p. 4).

While the modern Western psychological understanding of mindfulness does not simply adopt Buddhist notions, and although mindfulness is generally considered to be a natural human quality which can be cultivated with regular practice, it is important to acknowledge that secular mindfulness-based approaches have a strong grounding in Buddhist meditation. Within a Buddhist context, mindfulness has been described as:

> characterized by dispassionate, non-evaluative, and sustained moment-to-moment awareness of perceptible mental states and processes. This denotes continuous, immediate awareness of physical sensations, perceptions, affective states, thoughts and imagery"(Grossman, 2010, p. 88).

While these definitions emphasise that mindfulness encompasses more than 'just' attention, it is clear that attention plays a central role (Chiesa & Malinowski, 2011). How do these definitions fit in with your initial reflections?

We will touch on the scientific literature surrounding the nature of mindfulness and the established benefits of mindfulness training in Chapter 2, for those of you who are not overly familiar with the field. However, the purpose of this book isn't to tell you what mindfulness is, but rather to serve as an invitation to explore it for yourself. The material is aimed at those who provide some form of psychological therapy or support, but may be equally useful for those in a variety of helping professions, such as social workers, mental health project workers or medical practitioners. Equally, the material may also be useful for those who work in other capacities, such as educators.

Being a therapist is mentally and emotionally draining, regardless of whether you are 'freshly minted' or an 'old hand'. Research suggests that mindfulness training is beneficial for those in the helping professions and may serve as a useful self-care practice (Irving, Dobkin, & Park, 2009). There is some evidence that suggests that therapists who have trained in mindfulness may actually have better client outcomes, although the "jury is still out on this question" (Labbé, 2011, p. 30). The mindfulness for therapists programme presented in Chapter 3 includes a series of meditations and exercises to help you discover new ways of bringing your practice into your therapy room. Regular mindfulness practice supports the development of a decentred perspective, allowing you to step back and observe your attitudes, feelings and approaches to yourself and your client. Regular practice is absolutely essential and lies at the heart of all modern mindfulness training (Malinowski, 2008). Of course this is common sense – if you wanted to learn to play the piano you wouldn't expect to be able to play after only a couple of lessons! This fits in with the research, where there appears to be a relationship between the time individuals spent practising formal meditation and the levels of change observed in measures of mindfulness and well-being (Carmody & Baer, 2008). It might be useful to take a moment to reflect on whether you're really prepared to incorporate some regular practice into your life.

For those who use mindfulness therapeutically, this book offers a way to incorporate mindfulness practice into your working day. Several years ago, some of us offered training in MBSR for therapists. The participants were fascinated by the idea of mindfulness and MBSR, but they were really looking for the most useful exercises and approaches they could use with their clients immediately. While this may be appropriate in many therapeutic approaches, mindfulness is different in

3

that it is not possible to apply the 'see one, do one' approach. It takes time and practice to develop a personal experience and understanding of mindfulness, which is necessary before one can instruct others in an authentic way. If the support you provide for your clients as they begin to develop their own mindfulness practice is based on your own practice you are able to give a different quality of support and encouragement, rooted in a deep understanding of the difficulties encountered in mindfulness meditation.

Of course, we do not want to judge those of you who may have tried mindfulness exercises with your clients without practising yourself! Instead we would like to emphasise our view that in order to support your clients with their mindfulness practice credibly and successfully in the long term, it is essential that your guidance is rooted in your own practice.

As you work your way through this book you will be introduced to different practices which we hope will help you to develop and embed your personal mindfulness practice into your daily life. Recordings of all of the exercises are available online (see www.wiley.com/go/zarbock/mind fulnessfortherapists). Please see About the Companion Website at the back of the book for more details. The key types of practices are presented below.

Formal Mindfulness Exercises

These include meditations that focus on the breath, the body and mindful movement. Such formal exercises are usually practised regularly throughout the week. It is helpful to practise at least five times per week for a minimum of 20 minutes. It can be helpful to have an established place to practise, perhaps a corner of your study or bedroom. It is also useful to think ahead and plan a regular time to practise (e.g. in the morning before work, during lunch, etc.). Many people choose to attend some sort of group to support their practice and provide inspiration. Depending on your own preferences, you may find that attending a weekly yoga or Tai Chi class may suit you better than attending a meditation group.

Informal Mindfulness Exercises (Personal and Professional Lives)

These exercises help you to create moments of mindfulness in your everyday life. The book provides many suggestions as to how you can create such mini oases of mindfulness in your day. For example, you may choose to make the first few sips of your morning tea or coffee a mindfulness practice, or perhaps you could use the walk from your desk to the door as an opportunity to notice the pressure and weight of your feet on the floor, the changing pressure as you pick up your foot and the motion as you move your leg forward, ready to take your next step.

Therapist Role Mindfulness Exercises

These exercises centre on you and your role as a therapist. They aim to help you embed your mindfulness practice in your therapeutic work. For example, you may 'check in' with yourself before your client arrives, noticing bodily sensations or any thoughts or feelings which surface. During the session you may take a moment to check in with yourself again, noticing how you are sitting in your chair or the tone of your voice. There are many such examples throughout the book.

5

Joint Mindfulness Exercises

These joint mindfulness exercises have been designed to be done together with your client. The book includes several examples, such as the use of a joint breathing space or of short joint meditations as a way of closing a therapeutic session.

Intensive Exercises

Regular periods of intensive practice are a mainstay of most mindfulness training. If you are serious about your personal practice and bringing mindfulness into your lives, an intensive period of practice is highly recommended. Such periods can range from a single day to seven or ten days (or more). There are a variety of accessible retreats, from different traditions, which you might like to attend as you develop and expand your practice. For example, you might like to try a Vipassana, Zen or Yoga retreat. As the evidence mounts that mindfulness training is beneficial for therapists, it seems likely that there will be an increase in the support available specifically for therapists and those in the helping professions. We hope that this book will contribute to the ongoing growth and development of this field.

Client Exercises

We have also included a number of exercises which you can use with your clients. It is important that the decision to embark on these exercises is made jointly, as of course the client actually has to be willing to practise them if they are to have any impact.

Mindfulness and mindfulness training isn't a 'magic bullet' and won't make your problems or concerns disappear. However, it can help you engage with yourself and your clients in a more open, empathic way and provide a strong foundation to choose how you respond to events rather than simply reacting automatically. We hope that you enjoy exploring the material!

References

Carmody, J., & Baer, R. A. (2008). Relationships between mindfulness practice and levels of mindfulness, medical and psychological symptoms and well-being in a mindfulness-based stress reduction program. *Journal of Behavioral Medicine, 31*(1), 23–33.

Chiesa, A., & Malinowski, P. (2011). Mindfulness-based approaches: Are they all the same? *Journal of Clinical Psychology, 67*(4), 404–424.

Grossman, P. (2010). Mindfulness for psychologists: Paying kind attention to the perceptible. *Mindfulness, 1*(2), 87–97.

Hayes, S. C., & Wilson, K. G. (2003). Mindfulness: Method and process. *Clinical Psychology: Science and Practice, 10*(2), 161–165.

Irving, J. A., Dobkin, P. L., & Park, J. (2009). Cultivating mindfulness in health care professionals: A review of empirical studies of mindfulness-based stress reduction (MBSR). *Complementary Therapies in Clinical Practice, 15*(2), 61–66.

Kabat-Zinn, J. (1994). *Wherever you go, there you are: Mindfulness meditation in everyday life.* New York: Hyperion.

Labbé, E. E. (2011). *Psychology moment by moment: A guide to enhancing your clinical practice with mindfulness and meditation.* Oakland, CA: New Harbinger Publications.

Malinowski, P. (2008). Mindfulness as psychological dimension: Concepts and applications. *The Irish Journal of Psychology, 29*(1–2), 155–166.

2

Mindfulness

This chapter serves as a foundation to the more experiential approach taken in Chapters 3 and 4. Its purpose is not to provide an exhaustive literature review but rather a brief introduction to mindfulness. We will begin by addressing some of the pressures felt by therapists and how mindfulness can help, before taking a deeper look at what we mean by mindful awareness, the five elements of mindfulness and how they relate to one another. We will also reflect on how mindfulness relates to the first, second and third person perspective, and how this can impact you in your working day, be that alone or with your clients. Finally we will introduce mirror neurons and consider the role they may play in the therapeutic relationship.

Mindfulness for Therapists: Understanding Mindfulness for Professional Effectiveness and Personal Well-Being, First Edition. Gerhard Zarbock, Siobhan Lynch, Axel Ammann and Silka Ringer.
© 2015 John Wiley & Sons, Ltd. Published 2015 by John Wiley & Sons, Ltd.
Companion Website: www.wiley.com/go/zarbock/mindfulnessfortherapists

Burden on the Helper

What made you choose to work as a therapist? Whatever your reasons, the strain of supporting others may take its toll on your health and well-being. For a profession which focuses on supporting others it is somewhat ironic that there isn't a greater emphasis on supporting those of us who work as therapists or in helping professions (Morse, Salyers, Rollins, Monroe-DeVita, & Pfahler, 2012). The continuous professional use of empathy alongside the frequent exposure to emotionally difficult situations, such as demanding or violent clients, can leave those who work in the helping professions at risk of burnout (Paris & Hoge, 2010). Burnout is the end result of chronic overload, which is characterised by fatigue, anxiety, tension, a sense of reduced effectiveness, a drop in motivation and the prevalence of dysfunction, negativity, and cynical attitudes and practices. Fengler (2008) has described four key ways of relating to stressful situations which may increase your risk of burnout: high self-set goals, a limited understanding of your own ability, a denial of the impact of taking on a lot of work, and a permanent suppression of the fact that you are overloaded. Another explanation for the high levels of burnout amongst therapists is that regular exposure to negativity, suicidal thoughts, pessimism and self-destruction are extremely stressful and emotionally contagious. Does any of this sound familiar?

The unique therapist–client relationship approximates a close friendship or partnership in terms of emotional intimacy, yet is asymmetrical in many ways. For example, within your professional role there is an expectation that you are always friendly, tolerant and understanding, regardless of how you happen to be feeling. You do not receive the sort of reciprocal support from your clients that you would usually receive from friends and family. Rather, it is up to you to facilitate your own recovery and restore your own equilibrium at the end of every session. Learning to be sensitive to your own needs throughout your working day can support this process, while also helping you to notice your workload, stress levels and how these affect you. We feel that developing your own mindfulness practice and bringing it into your working day is one helpful way of doing this.

Mindfulness as Self-care

Building on the early work of Kabat-Zinn and colleagues, who used mindfulness to support chronic pain patients (1982; 1985), the last 30 years have seen a steady increase in the use of varying forms of mindfulness training to support clinical (Praissman, 2008) and healthy populations (Chiesa & Serretti, 2009). Mindfulness training can lead to reductions in stress, anxiety and depression, while improving health and well-being. There are a huge range of mindfulness training programmes available, many based on Mindfulness-Based Stress Reduction (MBSR), which has served as a template for other client-specific programmes such as Mindfulness-Based Cognitive Therapy (MBCT; Segal, Williams, & Teasdale, 2002) or Mindfulness-Based Eating (Kristeller & Hallett, 1999). Mindfulness plays an important role in pro-grammes such as Acceptance and Commitment Therapy (ACT; Hayes, Strosahl, & Wilson, 1999), where mindfulness is used to help create mental space, and Dialectical Behaviour Therapy (DBT; Linehan, 1993), where mindfulness helps to facilitate acceptance. Because of this growing interest, you may already be quite familiar with mindfulness!

As we mentioned in Chapter 1, in order to work with mind-fulness in a therapeutic context, we believe that having your own personal practice is essential. In the MBCT manual, the authors describe how they discovered this for themselves through trial and error (Segal et al., 2002). Given the popularity of mindfulness-based approaches this may seem like a burden at first. If you want to use mindfulness exercises with your clients you are placed in the position of either ignoring this advice and 'muddling along', or devoting additional time to developing your own practice. From this perspective, developing a mindfulness practice is all about being a 'good therapist' and helping others. A qualitative investigation of mindfulness training for therapists found that the majority of the participants chose to attend mindfulness training in the hope that it would help them be more compassionate and present with their clients (Irving et al., 2012).

Given the reported benefits of various forms of mindfulness training for a wide range of populations it isn't really surprising that mindfulness would be useful for therapists! If anything, it is surprising that there is comparatively little published on the topic – although that is changing rapidly. Mindfulness is coming to be considered an important self-care practice for those in the helping professions, which can be used to help reduce stress, anxiety and burnout (Escuriex & Labbé, 2011; Irving, Dobkin, & Park, 2009). Irving et al. (2012) conducted a qualitative investigation into the experiences of health care professionals who were enrolled in a mindfulness for a medical practice programme. They conducted a series of focus groups over two years with a total of 26 participants and have developed a working model of how mindfulness training is experienced by health care professionals. While they found many themes similar to those in clinical populations, they also observed that mindfulness training appeared to help the health professionals to become more aware of their own perfectionism, their need to 'fix' others and their automatic tendency to focus on the needs of others. This suggests that attending the programme resulted in deeper-level reflections about themselves and their approach to their work. Participants also felt that they became much more self-compassionate and had noticed a shift in their attitudes towards self-care practices.

While there is a paucity of long-term follow-ups with this population, a pilot evaluation of MBCT for clinicians did find that the majority of the participants were still practising mindfulness regularly 20 weeks after the end of the programme (de Zoysa, Ruths, Walsh, & Hutton, 2012). If these therapists didn't feel as though they were benefiting somehow it seems unlikely that they would still be practising so many months later! The benefits of mindfulness as a supportive tool for therapists is also supported anecdotally; for example, shortly after the 2011 earthquake in Christchurch, New Zealand, half of the counsellors and therapists present at a national training day reported that their own mindfulness practice had been their most useful coping tool (Miller, 2012). But how does it help?

Mindfulness and Self-awareness

Mindfulness, as understood from a modern Western psychological perspective (Siegel, Germer, & Olendzki, 2009), shares some similarities with theories of self-awareness, although they are not the same. Self-awareness involves directing your attention to your own ideals and standards, such as your personal values, goals and cultural and individual norms, which leads you to experience them more intensely. Increased self-awareness is also associated with higher levels of moral development. However, this may also result in you becoming more aware of any discrepancies between your 'self-aware' state and your usual state. In order to deal with this you may find yourself either working hard to minimise this discrepancy or to avoid it altogether as it is too uncomfortable. Hoyer (2000) would consider this a dysfunctional form of self-awareness, while functional self-awareness is coupled with confidence in one's own competence (self-efficacy). In this sense, mindfulness includes aspects of functional self-awareness.

Where self-awareness focuses purely on personal experience, mindfulness includes awareness of the wider world and is not completely self-focused. The assumption is that our attention jumps from one thing to another – often very quickly. In Asian tradition, this is described as 'monkey mind', which refers to monkeys who live in trees and are constantly jumping from branch to branch and tree to tree.

An important distinction between mindfulness and the concept of self-awareness is that mindful awareness is not reactive. Mindful awareness facilitates meta-cognitive insight, creating space to observe one's thoughts, feelings and actions (A. M. Hayes & Feldman, 2004; Teasdale, 1999). Thích Nhất Hạnh, who is a well-known Buddhist monk, describes how he experiences

this: "When we meditate, we seem to have two selves. One is the flowing river of thoughts and feelings, and the other is the sun of awareness that shines on them" (Hạnh, 1992, p. 13). The first step towards becoming more mindful is to become aware of your own monkey mind.

There is a strong aspect of 'non-judgment' in mindful awareness. Non-judgment can be best understood as non-reacting in emotional-motivational terms (Sauer, Lynch, Walach, & Kohls, 2011). Not judging yourself or your experience enables you to bring a fresh perspective to your environment, situation or self, as you have more cognitive and behavioural 'choices' (S. C. Hayes & Wilson, 2003). Mindful awareness is also associated with a positive, active form of acceptance. This is associated with acknowledging what is happening or how you are feeling and responding appropriately, rather than a sense of resignation, hopelessness and negative expectations for the future (Nakamura & Orth, 2005). So while self-awareness is an important aspect of mindfulness, there is much more to mindfulness than self-awareness.

The Five Elements of Mindfulness

As we mentioned in Chapter 1, there is no single, universally agreed-upon definition of mindfulness. We use the five-factor model proposed by Baer et al. (2006) as it is in keeping with our own experience of mindfulness. We have based the mindfulness for therapists programme around the development of these five facets of mindfulness:

1. Acting with awareness (which we have renamed 'concentration')
2. Observing
3. Describing
4. Non-reacting
5. Non-judging

Each of these facets is inter-related, as presented in the mindfulness circle (see Figure 2.1).

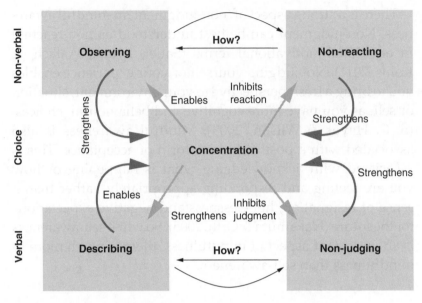

Figure 2.1 The Mindfulness Circle

Let's begin by taking a closer look at each of these five facets individually.

1. Concentration (acting with awareness)

Concentration involves being fully present in whatever you're doing. For example, when you're doing your regular food shopping, are you actually fully present in the supermarket? Are you paying

16

attention to what you're putting in your basket or is your mind somewhere else? When you're walking to work are you fully present as you make your journey or is your mind jumping from one thing to another, a bit like a monkey? It is rather sobering to acknowledge how much time you may actually spend in a sort of automatic pilot, disconnected from yourself and your environment. Mindfulness training can help you begin to tame your 'monkey mind' so that you can choose to pay attention and be fully present.

2. Observing

Mindful observance is linked to your awareness of the present moment and can be summed up as observing your own inner personal experiences, such as your thoughts or feelings, your experiences of the outer world, or sounds and smells. Remaining open and observing whatever is there addresses the often natural tendency for experiential avoidance of unpleasant stimuli or conditions.

Observing events, situations or objects in this way can also lead to a deeper understanding. For example, by observing one object carefully for a period of time, such as the changing sounds coming from an open window, you may become aware of subtle nuances in the bird songs, or perhaps notice a low sound, such as the rumble of a drill a few blocks away, which you hadn't noticed before. Mindfulness can work as a real world microscope, revealing aspects of yourself, and the world around you, which you may not have noticed otherwise.

3. Describing

This relates to naming whatever you perceive with simple words and descriptions. For example, imagine you are sitting in your living room and notice the sound of an aircraft. Your first instinct may be to label the sound as 'plane', because you know that the sound is associated with a plane. However, what you are actually perceiving is a noise which might be better labelled as 'noise', 'roar', 'thunder', or something similar.

4. Non-reacting

As mentioned already, learning to inhibit the tendency to react automatically to events is a key aspect of mindfulness. This includes physical, mental and verbal reactions. A powerful example of this automatic response is that of those with an attention deficit hyperactivity disorder (ADHD). Those with ADHD may react to even the slightest cues, resulting in often hasty and sometimes inappropriate behaviour. In hyperactivity there is often a non-directional

18

response in arousal situations or spontaneous motor activity is misplaced and must be inhibited. Non-responding involves the inhibition of impulses triggered by internal or external stimuli. So rather than reacting to thoughts or feelings it is easier to simply observe them and choose to let them go.

5. Non-judging

Evaluations are usually generated automatically in response to perceptual cues. Such perceptual impressions are immediately assessed. For example, 'I like/I do not like, pleas-

ant/unpleasant, good/evil, beautiful/ugly'. Generally, once you have made such an evaluation it tends to stick. From a mindful perspective, any verbal or mental characterizations should remain as close to the experience itself, rather than personal attitudes, thoughts, or feelings you may have. Mindfulness can help you become aware of these automatic responses, often for the first time, name them and then release them. Hence, while mindfulness doesn't stop the initial evaluations, it provides the opportunity to sidestep them (good/evil etc.), and subsequent thoughts and feelings which may spiral from them.

Relationships Between the Five Elements of Mindfulness

Now we have presented each of the five elements individually, let's take a closer look at the way they relate to one another by going back to the five-element circle of mindfulness. You will notice that concentration is central, since being aware of yourself and what you are doing in the present moment is a necessary foundation for all the other elements. As has already become obvious, concentration is not merely an element of mindfulness and attention, but also an element in the formation of purpose and intention, which is, essentially, verbally directed. Considering this from a psychological perspective, there are clear similarities with the formation of resolutions in autogenic training, to the inner directives in the Alexander Technique and the guiding principles of self-instruction in cognitive therapy. Each of the other four elements relates to qualities you can choose to bring to your present moment awareness. For example, in terms of observing, you can only observe the sights, sounds, thoughts or feelings which you are first aware of. Each of these four circular elements of mindfulness serves to support and reinforce one another and the central element of concentration.

In terms of developing your mindfulness practice, you may find the five-element circle of mindfulness a useful tool to help you reflect on how the different elements relate to one another and 'show up' in your practice. It may feel over-whelming (or even impossible) to bring each element to your practice consciously. It is quite a tall order to sit and meditate and try to be in the present moment, observing and naming what you experience without reacting or judging it. As you begin, it may be useful to work on developing these individual elements. As you do so you will discover the links naturally, at your own pace, rather than trying to 'force it'. As you begin you may find some natural pairings of the elements. For example, there is an obvious link between concentration and observation in the focused counting of your breath. Yoga exercises provide a good example of the link between non-reacting and observing. The exercises produce a mixture of physical relaxation and tension. Through observing the tensions, without reacting, they often resolve themselves. The link between non-judgment and describing could be prac-tised the next time you find yourself taking a walk around a park or a museum. You could choose to let any judgments float away and focus on what you perceive, perhaps naming some of the shapes or objects you encounter. Even if you just do this for a few minutes you will notice how strongly your experience is influenced by the verbal processes of naming and judging.

Mindfulness as Self-attunement

As you continue to develop and expand your own mindful-ness practice you may notice that you begin to take a more neutral stance with regard to your environment. This makes sense, given the non-judgmental and accepting attitudes which you are cultivating. If you are new to mindfulness, per-haps you are concerned that this neutrality may in fact be an 'escape hatch' in disguise, leading to either the avoidance or passive endurance of emotions such as shame, anger or sadness. In principle, it is possible for the incomplete practice of mindfulness to lead to this sort of distance from one's own emotions and needs.

However, this would only come from some key misunderstandings of mindfulness and mindfulness practice. Rather than being seen as creating this distance, mindfulness practice may help you to become more attuned to yourself and your needs. Drawing on developmental psychology and research into attachment Siegel (2007) argues that in your interpersonal relationships it is important that you are able to attune to the other person and have some sort of sense of them and their internal experience in order for them to 'feel felt', and vice versa. He then suggests that mindful awareness is actually a form of intra-personal attunement which helps you tune into thoughts, emotions and sensations. He also finds some striking similarities in the ways that interpersonal attunement and secure attachment appear to support well-being (D. J. Siegel, 2007).

From this perspective, mindfulness can be understood as a deep self-care practice in which you become more aware and secure with yourself by developing an internal resonance with your own states (emotions, impulses, thoughts, etc.). In turn, you are more able to open up and observe what is going on around you.

Mindfulness as a Flexible Change Between First, Second, and Third-person Perspective

First-person perspective

The first-person perspective is our subjective experience which is accessible only by ourselves. For example, your subjective impression of the colour green is only accessible to you. You will never know if someone else experiences the same green as you do when you use green to describe a lush summer meadow (Beckermann, 2008). Mindful awareness of this first-person perspective allows you to recognise that behind all your perceptions and experiences lies a sense of self, or 'I', who observes them. Hayes et al. (2003) distinguish between the

'self as context', which is our own self-conscious perception, and 'self-concept', which is a particular given object, or other perceptual cue. In meditative traditions this is described as the inner observer or the inner witness. For example, Luoma, Hayes and Walser (2009, p. 188) suggest: "The self, which we refer to is a comprehensive, timeless and connected sense of self, a context that includes all that you have experienced, but on the other hand, is not one of those experiences." During mindfulness practice you observe from the first-person perspective, behind the particular perceptions you may have, embracing a content-independent sense of self.

Second-person perspective

The second-person perspective develops when you bring your attention to the 'object', which is in this case another person. The second-person perspective could be described as the joining of two first-person perspec-tives, where their mutual experiences are built on their shared inter-subjectivity. It is not only interactive, but transactional. For example, my answer caused a reaction which in turn shaped my further response and so forth. So the personal experience of each is influenced by their interaction (De Quincey, 2000). A particularly powerful example of this is when two people fall head over heels in love with one another and because of their shared inter-subjectivity they feel as though they are living in a world of their own.

Mindfulness practice can create a second-person perspec-tive entirely in the spirit of Buber's approach (De Quincey, 2000). This means that your client does not feel as though he sits across from an 'omniscient' therapist as a 'sick' person, but rather that you are both two human beings with broadly similar life experiences such as failure and hope.

How does this relate to the five elements of mindfulness? We propose that concentration and observation take centre stage, as you focus on your client. We suggest that this space will help you to respond to your client in a consistent, natural way (encouraging phrases, gestures, posture) which will give your client the feeling of 'feeling felt' and understood. This could be supported by taking some time at the beginning of each session to do a short breathing practice together. This would help you to become more focused on your own experience, which in turn would lay the foundation for you to bring your attention to your client.

Third-person perspective

These days, the third-person perspective is predominantly associated with the objectifying approach of science (Kather, 2010), although we can bring the third-person perspective to the internalization of social rules, such as the "generalized other" (Mead & Morris, 1934). An example of this would be trying to see yourself through the eyes of others and endeavouring to meet their expectations.

In mindfulness practice, the use of language to describe your experience is one way of bringing this third-person perspective to your experience. It enables you to discuss your experience with others either verbally or in writing. If we dig deeper, we could argue that even the language you use to name your experiences internally, or

your 'self-talk', are part of the third-person perspective given that the language you use is culturally based.

The third-person perspective can also be observed in the natural tendency for our minds to sometimes 'run away' with us during our mindfulness practice, engaging in social story-telling as we replay events in our minds or imagine how things will unfold in the future, perhaps worrying how we will be perceived or thinking of what we will say to others. When you notice you have taken this perspective it is possible to choose to come back to the first-person perspective.

Another example of the third-person perspective in mindfulness practice is the way that deeply personal, inner experiences that occur during practice can foster the development of a deeper wisdom which can then be verbalised and utilised in the world. The concept of 'looking deeply', described by Thích Nhất Hạnh, can be used to understand in this sense of a third-person perspective. For example, a given sensory experience you have in the here and now (for example, your perception of a T-shirt) might lead you to contemplate what went into making that T-shirt and bringing it to you. Perhaps you might contemplate the origins of the cotton, the industrial processes which went into manufacturing the T-shirt, and the socio-cultural conditions involved.

The 'present now' is this morning, but also tomorrow's yesterday. In this knowledge-oriented variant of the third-person perspective of mindfulness, our experience of the present moment can either be the fruit of the past, or the root of a (possible) future. Thus, the time-space dimension is extended into the present moment and brought to life. To explore this perspective in more detail we have included practical exercises in Chapters 3 and 4.

All three perspectives are useful and meaningful in the context of mindfulness. Mindfulness can enable us to recognise which perspective is currently dominant, which, in turn, makes it easier to choose consciously which perspective we wish to take.

Mindfulness as a Conscious Choice of Self-focus

Even when not engaged in a particular task or activity, our minds are restless and tend to wander (Smallwood & Schooler, 2006). It has been suggested that this is the 'default mode of mind', where the brain is calm, yet still active. During such periods, which are defined by the absence of explicit internal or external stimuli that may prompt a response, individuals may experience so-called 'stimulus-independent thoughts' (SITs; Mason, et al., 2007) or 'task-unrelated thoughts' (TUTs; McKiernan, D'Angelo, Kaufman, & Binder, 2006).

It could be suggested that in the absence of concrete cognitive tasks the mind naturally switches to a self-narrative. Such stimulus-independent thoughts tend to be related to current issues, current goals, or worries and fears. The meaning or purpose of such a self-narrative can be interpreted in the sense of the consistency theory of Grawe (Grawe, 2004). From this perspective, self-narrative is a form of automatic 'consistency work', where your experiences during the day, memories, hopes, plans or desires work together to support your own self-image. Preserving your own sense of identity, avoiding discord and reducing tension are paramount. Since the verbal representations of this (what you tell yourself about yourself) play a big role in developing a coherent sense of self, this may be part of the reason why the mind falls into self-narrative so easily. At times this ongoing self-narrative can make it difficult to 'change the record'. How long has it been since you looked closely at those same old stories you tell

27

yourself? Whether you wish to change this self-narrative or not, mindfulness can help you to become more aware of it in a gentle, compassionate and sustainable way.

Reflecting on Mirror Neurons

There is a growing body of academic literature which explores the neural correlates of mindfulness (Chiesa & Serretti, 2010). Because the focus of this book is mainly experiential, we have chosen not to go into great detail regarding this material; however, we would like to take a moment to introduce you to mirror neurons and the role they may play at the intersection of mindfulness and your work as a therapist.

The discovery of mirror neurons (Rizzolatti & Sinigaglia, 2008) could be considered a revolution in our understanding of self-understanding. Until recently, it was thought that the brain nerve cells for the motor and sensory nerve cells of the sensory stimuli existed between areas associated with the different interconnected sensory modalities.

You are probably familiar with the sensory and motor homunculi, the distorted image of a human being which highlights how the nerves for movement and sensation are represented in the body (Bösel, 2006; Frith, 2009)? This image represents how your body works together so that you can see a cup of coffee, feel the warmth of the cup in your hand and smell it, all at the same time (Bösel, 2006). Adjacent to the motor neurons in the motor cortex are the pre-motor areas. It was previously thought that they were only involved in helping structure and co-ordinate complex movements. By coincidence, it was noticed that the pre-motor neurons (in monkeys) were activated even if the animal just observed someone making a movement to reach for something. This was contrary to expectation because the pre-motor cells were thought only to be responsible for the monkey's own movement (Rizzolatti & Sinigaglia, 2008). Further investigation revealed that these 'mirror neurons' respond similarly for other sensations, such as pain.

While the processing of visual cues and the actions of others is important in understanding others, the discovery of mirror neurons offers an elegant way of reflecting on the second-person perspective of mindfulness. The second-person perspective of mindfulness arises when two people (for the purposes of this book, you the therapist and your client) meet in a shared space. We introduced the importance of 'feeling felt' by the other person earlier, and mirror neurons appear to offer one such explanation for this resonance. So for example, A reflects the signals of B and B in turn reflects the reflected signals from A. This mirroring can be understood as an embodied empathy which helps us 'feel' for the other person. Mindfulness can help foster this by supporting present moment awareness to really observe the other person, in this case your client, and to be open to their experience, as an important first step.

Summary: Why Give Attention to Helping Professions?

There is a growing demand for therapists to be able to implement mindfulness-based approaches. Unlike some other approaches it is not possible to simply learn about mindfulness in order to teach others effectively – you must also understand it from your own personal practice. Further, it seems that mindfulness training may support the therapeutic alliance, with some studies suggesting that clients are more satisfied when working with clinicians who have developed a mindfulness practice. Finally, mindfulness training may support therapists personally and help them cope as they face the daily challenges of their work. Maintaining a mindfulness practice may seem arduous and almost over the top if your primary motivation is to be able to use it with your clients. But what if it could also help you to manage a gruelling schedule, difficult clients and the competing demands of home and family? In Chapter 3 we present an eight-week programme designed to help you develop a mindfulness practice and integrate it into your life.

References

Baer, R. A., Smith, G. T., Hopkins, J., Krietemeyer, J., & Toney, L. (2006). Using self-report assessment methods to explore facets of mindfulness. *Assessment, 13*(1), 27–45.

Beckermann, A. (2008). *Analytische Einführung in die Philosophie des Geistes. (3. Aufl.).* Berlin: de Gruyter.

Bösel, R. M. (2006). *Das Gehirn. Ein Lehrbuch der funktionellen Anatomie für die Psychologie.* Stuttgart: Kohlhammer.

Chiesa, A., & Serretti, A. (2009). Mindfulness-based stress reduction for stress management in healthy people: A review and meta-analysis. *The Journal of Alternative and Complementary Medicine, 15*(5), 593–600.

Chiesa, A., & Serretti, A. (2010). A systematic review of neurobiological and clinical features of mindfulness meditations. *Psychological Medicine, 40*(8), 1239–1252.

De Quincey, C. (2000). Intersubjectivity: Exploring consciousness from the second-person perspective. *Journal of Transpersonal Psychology, 32*(2), 135–156.

de Zoysa, N., Ruths, F. A., Walsh, J., & Hutton, J. (2012). Mindfulness-based cognitive therapy for mental health professionals: A long-term quantitative follow-up study. *Mindfulness,* 1–8.

Escuriex, B. F., & Labbé, E. E. (2011). Health care providers' mindfulness and treatment outcomes: A critical review of the research literature. *Mindfulness, 2*(4), 242–253.

Fengler, J. (2008). *Helfen macht müde: Zur Analyse und Bewältigung von Burnout und beruflicher Deformation.* Stuttgart: Klett-Cotta.

Frith, C. (2009). *Making up the mind: How the brain creates our mental world.* Oxford: Blackwell.

Grawe, K. (2004). *Neuropsychotherapie.* Göttingen: Hogrefe.

Hạnh, T. N. (1992). *Peace is every step: The path of mindfulness in everyday life.* New York: Bantam Books.

Hayes, A. M., & Feldman, G. (2004). Clarifying the construct of mindfulness in the context of emotion regulation and the process of change in therapy. *Clinical Psychology: Science and Practice, 11*(3), 255–262.

Hayes, S. C., Strosahl, K. D., & Wilson, K. G. (2003). *Acceptance and commitment therapy: An experiential approach to behavior change.* New York: Guilford Press.

Hayes, S. C., & Wilson, K. G. (2003). Mindfulness: Method and process. *Clinical Psychology: Science and Practice, 10*(2), 161–165.

Hoyer, J. (2000). *Dysfunktionale Selbstaufmerksamkeit.* Kröning: Asanger.

Irving, J. A., Dobkin, P. L., & Park, J. (2009). Cultivating mindfulness in health care professionals: A review of empirical studies of mindfulness-based stress reduction (MBSR). *Complementary Therapies in Clinical Practice, 15*(2), 61–66.

Irving, J. A., Park-Saltzman, J., Fitzpatrick, M., Dobkin, P. L., Chen, A., & Hutchinson, T. (2012). Experiences of health care professionals enrolled in mindfulness-based medical practice: A grounded theory model. *Mindfulness,* 1–12.

Kabat-Zinn, J. (1982). An outpatient program in behavioral medicine for chronic pain patients based on the practice of mindfulness meditation: Theoretical considerations and preliminary results. *General Hospital Psychiatry, 4*(1), 33–47.

Kabat-Zinn, J., Lipworth, L., & Burney, R. (1985). The clinical use of mindfulness meditation for the self-regulation of chronic pain. *Journal of Behavioral Medicine, 8*(2), 163–190.

Kather, R. (2010). Der Mensch – eine Einheit von Leib und Seele? Retrieved from http://www.akademieforum.de/grenzfragen/open/Grundlagen/Ka_Mensch/text.htm

Kristeller, J. L., & Hallett, C. B. (1999). An exploratory study of a meditation-based intervention for binge eating disorder. *Journal of Health Psychology*, 4(3), 357–363.

Linehan, M. (1993). *Cognitive behavioral treatment of borderline personality disorder*. New York: Guilford Press.

Luoma, J. D., Hayes, S. C., & Walser, R. D. (2009). *ACT-Training Handbuch der Acceptance & Commitment Therapie Ein Lernprogramm in zehn Schritten*. Paderborn: Junfermann.

Mason, M. F., Norton, M. I., Van Horn, J. D., Wegner, D. M., Grafton, S. T., & Macrae, C. N. (2007). Wandering minds: the default network and stimulus-independent thought. *Science, 315*(5810), 393–395.

McKiernan, K. A., D'Angelo, B. R., Kaufman, J. N., & Binder, J. R. (2006). Interrupting the 'stream of consciousness': An fMRI investigation. *Neuroimage, 29*(4), 1185–1191.

Mead, G. H., & Morris, C. W. (1934). *Mind, self, and society from the standpoint of a social behaviorist*. Chicago: University of Chicago Press.

Miller, J. H. (2012). Does the evidence that mindfulness-based interventions may assist counsellors and their clients post-earthquake stack up? *Counselling Psychology Quarterly, 25*(3), 339–342.

Morse, G., Salyers, M. P., Rollins, A. L., Monroe-DeVita, M., & Pfahler, C. (2012). Burnout in mental health services: A review of the problem and its remediation. *Administration and Policy in Mental Health and Mental Health Services Research, 39*(5), 341–352.

Nakamura, Y. M., & Orth, U. (2005). Acceptance as a coping reaction: Adaptive or not? *Swiss Journal of Psychology, 64*(4), 281–292.

Paris, M., & Hoge, M. A. (2010). Burnout in the mental health workforce: A review. *The Journal of Behavioral Health Services & Research, 37*, 519–528.

Praissman, S. (2008). Mindfulness-based stress reduction: A literature review and clinician's guide. *Journal of the American Academy of Nurse Practitioners, 20*(4), 212–216.

Rizzolatti, G., & Sinigaglia, C. (2008). *Mirrors in the brain: How our minds share actions and emotions.* Oxford: Oxford University Press.

Sauer, S., Lynch, S., Walach, H., & Kohls, N. (2011). Dialectics of mindfulness: Implications for Western medicine. *Philosophy, Ethics, and Humanities in Medicine, 6*(10).

Segal, Z. V., Williams, J. M. G., & Teasdale, J. D. (2002). *Mindfulness-based cognitive therapy for depression.* New York: Guilford Press.

Siegel, D. J. (2007). *The mindful brain: Reflection and attunement in the cultivation of well-being.* New York: WW Norton & Co.

Siegel, R. D., Germer, C. K., & Olendzki, A. (2009). Mindfulness: What is it? Where did it come from? In F. Didonna (Ed.), *Clinical handbook of mindfulness* (pp. 17–35). New York: Springer.

Smallwood, J., & Schooler, J. W. (2006). The restless mind. *Psychological Bulletin, 132*(6), 946.

Teasdale, J. D. (1999). Metacognition, mindfulness and the modification of mood disorders. *Clinical Psychology & Psychotherapy, 6*(2), 146–155.

3

Bringing Mindfulness Into Your Life

3.1 Week 1: Introduction to Mindfulness

Before we start, take a moment to check in with yourself. What body sensations are arising? What thoughts are going through your head? What emotions are you aware of? How are you feeling generally? For example, are you awake and motivated or tired and relaxed and a bit sceptical or curious, or something else? In a sense this is like taking an inventory of yourself. Just be aware of whatever presents itself to you. Whatever is there is neither good nor bad, it is simply what is there.

Mindfulness for Therapists: Understanding Mindfulness for Professional Effectiveness and Personal Well-Being, First Edition. Gerhard Zarbock, Siobhan Lynch, Axel Ammann and Silka Ringer.
© 2015 John Wiley & Sons, Ltd. Published 2015 by John Wiley & Sons, Ltd.
Companion Website: www.wiley.com/go/zarbock/mindfulnessfortherapists

Exercise 1: What is there?

The first exercise is primarily focused on the core element of 'concentration'. Take a moment to reflect on the last 24 hours. When have you been most attentive? When have you been least attentive? Checking in with yourself regularly is a useful tool. You will find that your least attentive moments were not entirely careless. If they were then you wouldn't recall them. Becoming aware of when you do not pay attention serves as a gateway, helping you to bring mindfulness into your daily life. This also helps you to become more aware during your mindfulness practice. Once you discover that your mind has wandered from the chosen anchor of attention – for example, your breath – you are able to let go of that gently and return your attention to the anchor. This is not to say that you will instantly become mindful 24 hours a day, but, over time, this tool will help you to become noticeably more aware.

Exercise 2: Breath concentration (5 minutes)

Take a moment to get into a relaxed posture and 'arrive'. You might like to sit on a chair with both feet planted firmly on the ground with a straight back. It is OK to lean on the back of your chair for some support but check that you're not slouched over. You can close your eyes or, if you prefer, you can leave them open, focusing on a spot on the floor in front of you where you feel your gaze can rest comfortably. Try to notice how this exercise affects you without giving yourself a hard time.

Now, turn your attention to the natural rhythm of your breath. There is no need to change anything, just observe any physical sensations you are aware of as you breathe in and out.

Focus your attention on the sensations in your abdominal area. Feel how your abdomen rises slightly when inhaling and lowers again as you exhale. Focus your attention on the sensations of breathing. If your attention wanders, take advantage of it! This isn't a 'failure', just part of the process of meditating. Use the opportunity to be aware of the distraction and then to let go of it and bring your attention back to your breath and the abdomen.

Do this exercise for five minutes. At the end of the five minutes bring your attention back to the room and slowly open your eyes (if you have chosen to close them).

Variation: For those new to mindfulness practice it may be helpful to place your palms over your lower abdomen. This can help you tune in to your breath as you feel the natural rise and fall of your abdomen. To intensify this, press your hands on your abdomen with each exhalation and then ease off as you breathe in. If this isn't suitable for you, just let your hands rest on your lap or on your knees.

Take a few moments to reflect on your experience of Exercise 2. Did your mind wander much? When it wandered, were you able to take a benevolent stance and return your attention to the exercise? Were there any similarities and/or differences between these short exercises in 'concentration' and the concentration you need in everyday life?

It is unlikely that you would have managed to keep your attention on your breath continuously during this exercise – it is not as simple as it sounds! You probably found that your mind drifted off after a few breaths. This is entirely normal, especially for beginners. Many practitioners find that as they close their eyes, their mind wanders very quickly. This is the starting point for any mindfulness training, and is no reason to be discouraged in terms of 'performance'! Quite the contrary! This is where the value of regular practice comes in and the difficulties you perceive are an indispensable learning tool. The 'core' of mindfulness consists of the perception and recognition of what is happening in the present moment. This includes, in particular, the perception and recognition of the difficulties in the practice of mindfulness.

Finding your position

Unlike the everyday process of sitting, when you sit for meditation it is helpful to take a moment to find a stable position. Exercise 3 will help you find the right position for you.

Exercise 3: Finding your 'relaxed, upright position' (5 minutes)

For this exercise, please sit in an upright position. If you wish to sit on a chair, place both feet firmly on the ground in

front of you. If your feet don't touch the ground you might like to place some cushions or blankets underneath your feet to help you become more stable. Your hands can either sit loosely on your thighs, or be placed together in your lap, whatever feels comfortable. If

you wish to sit on a cushion, try taking a kneeling position then sit back on your cushion. Try to position yourself so that both knees touch the ground. This relieves pressure on the hips. Don't worry if your knees don't reach the ground (yet), you can use small pillows/ blankets to fill the gap. Aim to sit on the front third of the chair or cushion.

Your skeleton should be aligned so that body weight is supported mainly by your sitting bones as your muscles can only relax if they don't have to carry all of the weight of your body. Otherwise they may become stiff, which may lead to pain or discomfort during meditation. Once seated, take about five minutes to find your own perfect 'relaxed upright position'. Perhaps you notice that your upper body is leaning forward slightly, or maybe just parts of it (e.g. the upper or the lower spine)? Maybe you are aware of some areas of tension? Everyone is different, so when experimenting with finding the right posture for you, please move gently and be conscious of what is comfortable for you. You might like to tilt your pelvis gently forwards and backwards very slightly until you find a place in the middle where you feel secure and upright. While it is important to find the right posture at the beginning, please note that you are still free to move and adjust your posture throughout all of the meditations. Meditation does not need to be static!

Exercise 4: Seated mindfulness (5–10 minutes)

If you are still in the seated position outlined in Exercise 3, stay there.

If not, take a few minutes to resume the position. You are now going to scan your body, focusing on each area in turn. Start by taking a moment to notice the weight of your body, resting on your sitting bones on the chair or cushion and any other places where your body makes contact with the chair/cushion or the ground. You might like to have a little move around and adjust your posture at this point.

When you're ready, bring your attention to your feet. Really take the time to notice the weight of your feet on the ground or cushion, any warmth or coolness, any sensations such as tingling, and any thoughts or emotions which arise. No particular sensation or thought is 'wrong'. If you don't notice anything, that is fine too. Then continue scanning your body in this way, moving upwards towards your head. If you're distracted by thoughts or feelings try not to give yourself a hard time. It is perfectly OK! Rather than trying to push the thoughts or feelings away, try letting them be there for a moment and then choose to release them gently. There is a subtle, yet powerful, difference. For example, if you notice any tension in certain muscle areas then just try to notice it, perhaps saying 'this is tension' or 'tension' to yourself. If you have the impulse to try and change something, just notice it, name it and try to let go of your evaluations of it.

When you have 'visited' each body region, you might like to take a moment to notice your body as a whole. How does it feel? Then rest in your body for a few moments. Try this for five to ten minutes, opening your eyes when you are ready.

When you have finished the exercise take a moment to notice what experiences you had. What thoughts emerged? What impulses did you observe? How did you deal with each of these observations? Could you name them and release them without reacting to them? Or have you let yourself be tempted by the 'monkeys'?

Notice how you responded!

Regular practice

In order to integrate mindfulness into your life, you will need to practise regularly. We suggest that you find a consistent place to practise as it will help you to get into a meditative state more quickly. It doesn't need to be a large room; even a quiet corner of your living room or office would work. We suggest that you decide whether you wish to use a chair or a meditation cushion. Perhaps you could go into a shop and try a few meditation cushions to see what you think of them before you invest in one. It is well worth spending some time to find the right posture for you. When you are in the right position you will feel supported and stable when sitting.

In order to integrate mindfulness gradually into your life we have put together a number of exercises for you to practise each week. We've divided the exercises into two areas:

1. Regular practice which will guide you throughout this course.
2. Specific exercises which focus on the aspect of mindfulness you have been reading about.

Exercise 5: Flash mindfulness (3–5 minutes)

The first regular practice we would like to introduce is flash mindfulness. Do this three times daily (e.g., 08:00, 12:00, 16:00). It is useful to think through when this short flash mindfulness

41

practice would fit into your day best. It may even be that this changes depending on your schedule. Make a plan for the coming week and set some sort of reminder for yourself – perhaps on your phone or on your computer. There are plenty of free meditation timers available online.

Before you start, note the answers to the following questions:

1. How strong is the tension in my body? (0–100%)
2. What emotions are in the foreground?
3. What thoughts are in the foreground?

Now turn your attention to your breathing for five inhalations and exhalations.

Next, put your attention on your body, starting with the sensations in your hands, down to the fingertips ... then in the forearms, upper arms ... in the forehead and scalp, the eyes ... the nose ... the lips, cheeks and jaw muscles ... in the neck and shoulders ... the whole back ... in the tummy, the buttocks ... in the thighs ... in the lower legs and feet, to the toes. Then let your focus become wider and turn your attention to your body as a whole. Repeat this body awareness in waves a few times until you feel that you have a good appreciation of your body in the present moment.

Mindfulness diary

Throughout the coming weeks we suggest that you keep a mindfulness diary. This is a way of reflecting on your experience of the practices and of integrating them into your life. The notebook can be in whatever format suits you best (hardcopy, electronic, etc.). Take a moment to make an entry in your first mindfulness diary. Reflect on your observations from this first session. What have you noticed? Perhaps a curiosity has emerged? Are you motivated to keep going?

Exercises for the week ahead

- Exercise 5: Flash mindfulness (three times daily).
- Mindfulness diary (daily).
- Exercise 2: Breath concentration (daily, minimum of five minutes).
- Exercise 4: Seat mindfulness (daily, minimum of five minutes).

Please do explore the online materials that support the material presented in this chapter: www.wiley.com/go/ zarbock/mindfulnessfortherapists

3.2 Week 2: The Five Elements of Mindfulness

Let us begin by taking a short personal inventory. How do you feel right now? What body sensations arise? What thoughts are going through your head? What kind of emotions are you currently experiencing? How is your general health? Are you awake and motivated, or perhaps a little tired? As you observe yourself remember that whatever you notice is simply what is there right now, it is neither good nor bad.

Take a moment to reflect on the entries in your mindfulness practice diary. How did you find the daily practice? Was it always easy to motivate yourself? Have there been moments when you were tempted to skip your mindfulness practice? This may even have happened a few times. If you haven't practised as much as you wanted to, just be aware of it and choose to make it a priority in the remaining weeks.

Contents of the second week

In this session you will become more familiar with the elements of mindfulness and get practically acquainted with, and prepare for, the beginning of the third week of meditation exercises. Following on from the practice of observation and concentration in the last unit, we start this unit with the first asana yoga practice, Exercise 6, Pre-tree (a fuller discussion of asana yoga is provided in Week 6).

Exercise 6: Pre-tree (5 minutes)

Begin by standing in a relaxed, upright position. To find the right position for yourself, you might like to take a moment to shift your weight around slightly. Once you are ready, shift your weight onto your left foot and gently lift your right foot, placing the right foot so that it is touching the top of the left foot. This is a gentle introduction to yoga balances. Don't worry if you find this difficult at first, many people do! Hold this position for two minutes if you can. Then place your right foot back onto the floor and stand with weight equally distributed on both feet on the floor for a moment. Notice if anything has changed. Then shift your weight onto your right foot and gently lift your left leg, placing your left big toe on top of your right big toe and again hold this for two minutes. After two minutes put your left foot back onto the ground and, again,

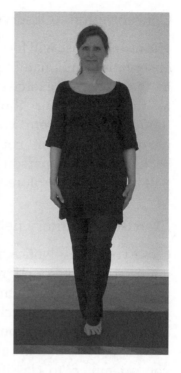

take a few moments to stand with both feet firmly on the ground. Take a few breaths in that position, just noticing how that feels.

What did you experience during the exercise? When the mind is challenged by a new job it is relatively easy to stay focused. As soon as the job is no longer a challenge the monkey mind begins to wander! In this exercise the threat of losing your balance provides very prompt feedback that your mind might be beginning to wander. The threat of losing your balance requires your mind to return to the present moment immediately. In everyday life, this feedback is often not so clear. Regular mindfulness practice helps you become more aware, while at the same time remaining focused for longer periods of time.

Concentration – Observing – Naming

The next exercise will focus on the elements of concentration, observation and naming. As you will have experienced in the previous exercises, in meditation the mind tends to return to your thoughts, again and again. These thoughts arise from your experience. This first-person perspective is, of course, influenced by your own background and personal history. The following exercise will help you to explore this.

Exercise 7: Auditory field (10 minutes)

Close your eyes. Notice any sounds that are present. Try to interpret just the sound, not the activities, objects or individuals you associate with them. For example, rather than labelling a sound as 'motorcycle' or 'car', try labelling it as a 'noise' or 'hum'. Do this for about ten minutes.

How did you find the exercise? Were there any sounds that you attempted to classify mentally? Perhaps some of the sounds evoked memories or other thoughts? Do you have any ideas about everyday situations in which this exercise could be carried out? In principle this exercise works in most situations – whether you are taking your morning shower, on the bus to work, eating lunch, and so forth.

Non-judging

In the last exercise you may have noticed that, almost involuntarily, you judged the sounds you heard. For example, a buzz may have been an 'annoying buzz', or a chirp may have been a 'shrill chirp'. Even if this didn't happen during the exercise, it is likely that you do label sounds in this way in your daily life. Mindful perception includes evaluating the content of perception without all these automatic judgments and labels. The following exercise will help you experiment with this.

Exercise 8: Non-judgmental description (15–20 minutes)

For the following exercise we recommend either enlisting the help of a second person or using a recording device. If you are working with another person, sit facing each other. Begin by facing your counterpart and describe them non-judgmentally. Try to remain as abstract and elementary as possible. It might help to pretend that you're an extraterrestrial who has just landed on earth and is looking at a human being for the very first time. While it would be natural for humans to describe parts of the body such as arms, shoulders or faces, what would an alien say? A human might simply describe someone as having a mouth, but an alien who had never seen a human before might describe the mouth in much more detail, perhaps as a long horizontal recess around five inches long. Keeping this in mind, look carefully at your partner and note what you see.

If you want to do this exercise alone, sit in front of a mirror and start your recording device. Describe your face clearly, remembering to take a non-judgmental stance and describe what you see. If you notice that you are evaluating yourself, try and rephrase your statement. Try to remain as abstract and elementary as possible.

You might like to try a variation of this. Sit in front of a window and describe what you see looking out of it. Do this exercise for at least 15 minutes. If you have been practising with another person you can take a few minutes to reflect on your experiences of the exercise with your partner. If you did the exercise on your own, listen to your recording straight away and reflect on the process.

You may be surprised at the number of judgments that popped up automatically. There is no reason to worry about this as such assessment processes are commonplace and often serve a useful function. They allow us to distinguish what we wish to pay attention to. This, in turn, allows us to avoid those things we do not wish to pay attention to. For example, someone who is looking for a new relaxation CD in a music store and sees the 'Rock' section may react automatically with judgments such as 'loud' or 'deafening'. However, upon seeing the 'Meditation' section, they may react with judgments such as 'pleasant' or 'soothing'. However, if a month later the same person is planning a surprise party for his friends who love rock music, the same headings may evoke very different judgments. For example, 'Rock' may now be judged as 'good times' or 'party', while 'Meditation' may now be judged as 'boring' or 'slow'.

While these evaluations, or judgments, are commonplace, they are also often automatic. Although they may be helpful at times, this is not always the case. Exercise 8 may help you to become aware of this and help you to interrupt these automatic judgments when appropriate. For example, you may recall we mentioned that a risk criterion for the development of burnout is assessing a situation as stressful. However, taking a non-judgmental approach enables you to look at precisely what is happening in that situation and how you feel about it and how you are responding to it. This is empowering and enables positive action to be taken. In the coming weeks try this out for yourself and notice how you evaluate different situations, people and your own body signals.

Exercise 9: Short meditation (5–10 minutes)

For today's final exercise you need a standard clothes peg. Take a relaxed, upright sitting position and place the clothes peg either on your lap or on the floor or table in front of you. Focus your attention on the clothes peg for the next few minutes. Try to let go of the label of 'clothes peg', and imagine you were seeing it for the very first time and had no idea what it was. For example, terms such as 'square' or 'gap in middle' may come to mind. Just notice all of the new labels for this item which spring to mind. When you feel as though you have described all the relevant features, stop trying to label them and just focus on the peg as a whole. If you notice that your mind has wandered just be aware of that without judgment and bring your attention back to the clothes peg. Do this exercise for about five to ten minutes. As an alternative to the clothes peg you could practise with other simple household objects such as a spoon, Lego brick, cereal bowl, match, and so forth.

Now take a moment to reflect on this exercise. How did the four elements of mindfulness come together? Did you notice the integration consciously? What can you conclude from your past experience of mindfulness practice?

Exercises for the week ahead

- Exercise 5: Flash mindfulness. For the rest of the programme expand the Flash mindfulness exercise by asking yourself: What was my most attentive moment of the day? What was my most careless moment of the day? What physical sensations were evoked in each of these moments? (three times daily).
- Mindfulness diary (daily).

- Exercise 7: Auditory field (three times in the week, minimum of five minutes). You might like to practise Exercise 7, or the Flash mindfulness exercise, in the relaxed sitting position (see Week 1, Exercise 3). This will help you to prepare for the sitting exercises next week.
- Exercise 8: Non-judgmental description (three times in the week, minimum of 15 minutes).

Have fun practising!

3.3 Week 3: Integrating Mindfulness into Everyday Life

Take a moment to stop and reflect: how does your body feel? What sensations are you aware of? What thoughts are going through your head right now? What emotions are you aware of? How is your general health? Just notice whatever presents itself to you.

Now take a moment to review your mindfulness diary for the last week. What do you notice? Did you manage to practise regularly? Do you feel encouraged to practise more? Have you noticed any situations where your mindfulness practice has impacted your daily life? You might like to renew your commitment to your meditation practice for the week ahead.

Contents of the third week

This section will introduce you to some basic formal mindfulness techniques and present some ideas about how you can integrate mindfulness into your life.

We will begin with a pre-awareness exercise from yoga which can help promote alertness and clarity of mind during formal meditation and may prevent you from dozing off or slipping into a daydream. This exercise is especially useful first thing in the morning before your meditation. If you perform this exercise at other times make sure you wait at least three hours after eating. If you have high blood pressure please do not practise this exercise without your doctor's permission.

Exercise 10: Energise (15 minutes +)

Stand on the ground with your back straight. Open your legs hip-width apart. Make sure that your feet are parallel and your knees slightly bent.

Part 1: Take a few slow deep breaths and expel all the air from your lungs. Then take a gentle breath, filling your lungs with air until they are about three-quarters full. Lean slightly forward with your arms resting on your thighs, support-ing you. Your head should remain in line with your spine. Breathe out and pull your abdomen towards the spine and hold your breath for a moment. Slowly stand up as you inhale.

Do this sequence three times, breathing gently for a few moments in between.

Part 2: Breathe in and out for a few moments, only filling your lungs two-thirds full each time. Stand with your feet on the ground parallel to one another. Place your arms on your thighs, keeping your head in line with your spine. Breathe out, expelling all the air from your lungs and hold your breath. Then, before you inhale again, push your stomach in and out quickly for a few moments. Then as you inhale, straighten your back and stand up. Do this three times, taking a few moments to breathe normally between repetitions.

Part 3: Take a few deep breaths, ensuring that your lungs are only two-thirds full. This time keep the air in your lungs and hold your breath. Gently tap your fingertips on your upper chest and neck. If you like you can also tap your neck and shoulders. When you need to take a breath, breathe in quickly and breathe out in a short burst. Then, holding your breath, lean slightly forward and place your hands on your thighs, supporting your weight, remembering to keep your head in line with your spine. Pull your stomach in towards your spine. Hold this for a few moments and then release and breathe normally for a few moments.

Part 4: Finally, keep your arms at your sides and turn your palms outwards. Gently raise your arms up as you inhale with your hands touching at the top of your head as you finish inhaling. When you are in that position, clasp your hands above your head and slowly bend your body to the right and then come up to the centre. Repeat this on the left side and then come back to the centre. Lower your hands in parallel as you exhale. When you finish exhaling, your hands should be beside your body once again. Repeat this sequence at least twice.

When you have finished these exercises take a moment to notice how you feel. Are there any subtle changes in your body? Part 4, in particular, is a useful exercise if you feel you have run out of energy and can be used at any time. If you are using this exercise to re-energise, it might be useful to imagine your energy reserves being 'refuelled' as you inhale and spreading throughout your body as you exhale. This exercise is also useful after a period of prolonged sitting (such as in a training session, lecture, or therapy session).

Meditation

Meditation, in one form or another, exists in most spiritual traditions. In Buddhism, meditation is undertaken with the aim of developing mental calm, clarity and compassion, in order to develop insight and wisdom. It is important to consider that while there may be many formal meditations, any activity can be considered a meditation. It is not the activity per se, but rather the attitude that one takes towards it that makes it meditation.

There are various forms of formal meditation. You will be introduced to some of them in the following weeks. We do not suggest that you try and incorporate all of these into your daily practice at once. You are probably familiar with the phrase 'Jack of all trades but master of none'. Rather than becoming a 'Jack of all meditations' we suggest you choose one form of formal meditation practice, which feels right to you, and then practise that regularly. Of course this does not mean you can't incorporate other meditations into your practice, but it might be helpful for you to pick one meditation which you will commit to, to practise regularly.

Building on your experiences thus far, we will now introduce one of the basic mindfulness meditations, the sitting meditation.

Exercise 11: Sitting meditation (10 minutes)

Take a relaxed upright sitting position. Begin by breathing in and out through your nose, just observing your breath. Do not try to change your breath in any way. If it is difficult for you to breathe through your nose then breathe through your mouth instead. After observing the natural rhythm of your breath for a few moments, become aware of it as it moves through three body regions: the nose, the upper chest or heart region and the abdomen. See if you can become aware of the cool air flowing in through your nose as you inhale. Continue to follow the respiratory movements produced in the body and observe how the upper and lower rib cage expands and the abdomen rises. When you are ready to exhale, watch as the lower abdomen falls and then notice the ribcage follow suit. Perhaps you can feel the inside of the nostrils, as the air, warmed by body heat, flows out again. Your attention follows each inhalation and exhalation. If you notice that your mind wanders, just make a mental note of this without giving yourself a hard time for becoming distracted. Then just let go of these distractions and return your attention to your breath. If this happens repeatedly just continue to notice them and let them go, returning your attention to your breath.

Variation – Counting the breath: Many people find the sitting meditation difficult to start with as they are not able to concentrate for ten minutes. If ten minutes is too much for you then this exercise may help. It is particularly useful for beginners, although, of course, it is good for experienced practitioners too! Instead of focusing on the breath, in this variation, the practitioner breathes in and out naturally, counting each exhalation up to ten, so the first exhalation being '1'. After the 'counted' exhalation enjoy a moment of silence and tranquillity. Breathe in naturally when if feels right and then continue to count each exhalation. When you get to ten, start again with one and repeat for ten minutes.

If that's still too little support, you can count the inhalation and the exhalation. So you would count '1' for the first inhalation, '2' for the following exhalation, '3' for further inhalation and '4' for the following exhalation and continuing on until you reach '10'. Then start again with '1' for the next inhalation. Remember to take ten minutes for this exercise.

Another option: Another variation is to label each inhalation and exhalation with a word such as 'ON' when inhaling and 'OFF' when exhaling, or 'HERE' on the inhalation and 'NOW' as you exhale.

Take a moment to reflect on your experience of the sitting meditation. How did you find it? Which of the five elements of mindfulness (concentration, observing, describing, non-judging, non-reacting) were you aware of in the exercise? At what points did you find your mind wandering? How did you deal with these distractions? Did you follow the impulse to think about the distraction? Did you feel frustrated or resentful of the distraction? Or perhaps you were simply able to notice you were distracted, let go of it and return your attention to the exercise?

Non-reacting

Successful non-reacting involves accepting distractions and impulses as they arise, and then choosing not to respond to them. For example, imagine you are lying in the bathtub, relaxing after a long and tiring day. Suddenly your mind starts running through a list of tasks you should have completed before you left the office. Do you run over these tasks while you are in the bath and make them the focus of your attention? Or do you register the tasks and continue to enjoy your bath, feeling the warmth of the water as you let your body relax, knowing that once you are finished your bath you can decide what, if anything, you need to do. Regular meditation can help you strengthen your ability to step back from thoughts and impulses and choose how you wish to respond to them. This is the fifth element of mindfulness.

Integration of mindfulness into everyday life

We hope that by this point in the programme you will have come to see that integrating mindfulness into your daily life is essential if you wish to reap the rewards of mindfulness practice. In addition to the Flash mindfulness exercises there are numerous ways you can integrate mindfulness into your daily life. Please take the time to think about how you can bring a meditative stance to some of your daily activities. When and where can you integrate mindfulness into your life? Here are a few examples which may help:

- When you get into the shower, notice as the first drops of water make contact with your body. Which parts of your body does the water fall on first? Perhaps different parts of your body are more sensitive to the temperature than others? Notice how you're standing – do both feet make contact with the ground? If not, which parts are off the ground? Are you standing straight or are your legs angled? Perhaps your knees are slightly bent? As you continue with your shower, you might like to notice the different smells and sensations as you use any soaps or shampoos.
- You could also choose to use your next snack or meal as an opportunity to practise mindfulness. Begin by sitting or standing with a straight back and notice the smell of the food, the way your body reacts and the temperature and taste of the food as it enters your mouth (for more information please see Exercise 28 in Chapter 3.9).
- Become aware of your posture while you're driving. You might like to take a moment to notice the position of your hands on the wheel and to notice any tension in your body as you hold the wheel. Does your back touch your seat or do you lean slightly forward?
- The next time you are mopping or vacuuming the floor you could notice how you hold the mop or vacuum. Where are your hands? How do you feel about the task? Are you working quickly or taking your time?

Hopefully this short list will have sparked your creativity and you can see how easily you can bring mindful awareness into your everyday life. Most people find it easier to pay attention when engaged in an activity they consider pleasant, such as eating something they enjoy. Other less pleasurable activities, such as doing the washing up, may be more difficult for some people. Mindfulness practitioners have the opportunity to side-step this sort of evaluation and be fully present in whatever activity they are engaged in without judging it. The aim of this section isn't to encourage you to dissect every aspect of your daily routine, rather it aims to encourage you to become more mindful in your daily life. As a starting point, you might like to try Exercise 12, the mindful tea exercise.

Exercise 12: Everyday mindfulness 'tea' (20 minutes +)

Take the next 20 minutes or so to prepare and drink your tea. What is your very first task? Do you need to consider which tea to drink, or do you have an established favourite? Do you use loose tea or teabags? Do you use a teapot or do you prefer to make your tea directly in your cup? At what point do you fill and boil the kettle? Pay close attention to your posture as you begin, and continue the exercise. As the kettle boils, notice when you're ready to pick it up and pour it into the teapot or cup. As you pick up the kettle notice how heavy it feels. As you begin to pour the water, notice if any steam escapes from the spout. Then, as you pour the water, notice the sound of the water as it leaves the spout, along with the changing weight of the kettle as it becomes lighter. What is your posture like? What physical reactions do you experience as you smell the aroma of the tea brewing? Watch the changing water as it becomes darker the longer the tea is left to brew. Maybe you can even perceive changes in the intensity of the aroma. When you want to remove the tea from the water what movements do you make? Watch closely as the last drops of tea fall from the strainer or teabag. Perhaps you notice ripples on the surface of the tea as these last drops hit the surface of the water. How long do these ripples remain visible? As you sit, observing your tea, be aware of your posture, your physical reactions and your impulses. If the tea is in a teapot, gently pour it into your cup, observing the process as before.

When you feel the tea is ready to drink, notice the movements of your body as you reach out, pick up your cup and bring it to your lips. Slowly taste the tea with your tongue before taking your first full sip. Let the tea sit in your mouth for a moment as you focus on the taste. Notice if the temperature is comfortable, perhaps different parts of your mouth are more sensitive? Does the flavour change over time? Notice when you're ready to swallow the tea. How long does the taste remain in your mouth after you have swallowed it? Now take your second sip of tea and this time, swirl it around your mouth. Notice how you do this. Do you swirl randomly, clockwise, anti-clockwise or in some other pattern? Observe which muscles appear to be used. Continue drinking your tea and noticing your various movements, the taste of the tea, your posture and your thoughts.

This exercise should take at least 20 minutes to complete.

After finishing your tea drinking exercise, stop for a moment and reflect on the experience. How did you find the exercise? Did anything surprise you? What did you notice about the tea?

Of course we don't suggest that you approach every cup of tea this way! However, the exercise serves as a reminder that any activity can be used as a form of informal mindfulness practice. It's not about becoming 'perfectly attentive', but rather becoming gradually more aware of the present moment.

Exercises for the week ahead:

- Exercise 5: Flash mindfulness (three times daily).
- Mindfulness diary (daily).
- Exercise 11: Sitting meditation (three times in the week).
- Make time to observe daily activities/situations in a focused and non-judgmental way. Do this three times per day. Here are some examples from participants at our mindfulness

courses. Together, we have assigned them to elements of mindfulness.

Concentration
- Focus on what you hear (see Exercise 7).
- Perception of a (different) sensory channel focus.

(Concentrated) observing
- Mindful walking. Make the act of walking the focus of your attention. For example, notice how you lift your leg and move it forward, how it feels as you place your foot on the ground and how the muscles in your body are supporting you.
- Mindful tea/drink making (see Exercise 12).
- Look at the window and really notice what is there.
- Mindful driving. Focus on the environment you are driving through, the road, other motorists, and so forth.
- Mindful speaking/listening to others. For example, the sound of the voice, the content of the communication, and so forth.
- Brushing your teeth or applying makeup.
- Cloud watching.

Describe (concentrated observing)
- Label your thoughts and feelings.

Non-judgment (concentrated observing)
- Thoughts and feelings of acceptance.

Non-responding (concentrated observing)
- Let go of road rage. Choosing not to become angry or curse if you are stuck in a traffic jam or if another driver irritates you.

We hope that you find these exercises useful!

3.4 Week 4: Mindfulness as a Way of Life

Begin by checking in with yourself. How are you right now? How is your body? What sort of emotions are you experiencing? How are your energy levels? Remember to observe whatever you notice without judgment.

When you are ready, turn to your mindfulness diary and review the entries for the past week. What do you notice? What motivated you to practise? Were there any particular things that distracted you? How much formal meditation did you do? How was that? How did you find the informal practice? When do you plan to practise in the coming week?

Contents of the fourth week

In this session we will focus on the fifth aspect of mindfulness, non-reacting. We will also expand your experience of formal and informal mindfulness exercises.

Automatic pilot and non-reacting

In the first week you were asked to keep a record in your mindfulness diary of moments when you felt you had been careless in your day. Take a moment now to look over your mindfulness diary and think about these careless moments. Why do you describe them as careless? How did they come about? How do you feel about the fact that you weren't totally in the present moment?

Automatic pilot in everyday life

As you will have realised by now, assuming 'autopilot mode' – that is non-reflective behaviour based on long, monotonous and habitually performed actions and reactions – complicates the practice of mindfulness. For example, do you always put the water in your coffee cup before the milk, or vice versa? You may have established such daily rituals because they served a particular purpose. However, such habitual patterns of behaviour, acted on automatically, do not allow room for mindful awareness. There are clearly benefits to such patterns, but there are also drawbacks. Perhaps there is now a quicker, more efficient way of completing your task? Often such behaviours are only interrupted when outside events force a change. Informal mindfulness practice allows you to take a step back from such habitual behaviour and look at the situation with fresh eyes. To explore some of your automatic behaviours in more depth, pick a regular daily activity that you engage in without really needing to think about it. Next time you engage in that activity try to bring your awareness to each individual action, the pauses between actions and the plans you make for your next action. This exercise may help you to reflect on the difficulties your clients may experience as they try and change certain behaviours or thought patterns.

Can automatic pilot be useful?

In order to explore whether or not automatic pilot can be useful, let us begin by using the example of driving a car. When you first learn to drive, it takes your total concentration as you put your foot on the clutch, move the gear, then gently ease off the clutch as you transfer the pressure to the accelerator.

With experience, these activities gradually become automatic and you find that you are able to listen to music or chat to passengers with ease, all the while ready to respond to the demands of the road. If drivers weren't able to make such moves automatically, then driving would be a very demanding, not to mention dangerous, experience! This sort of automatic behaviour is by no means limited to driving. The much vaunted skill of 'multi-tasking' aims to use such automatic behaviours to our advantage. However, there are limits as to what can be attended to at any particular moment.

Given how many of us are burned out and overwhelmed by the sheer volume of work we have to manage, and the expectation that we juggle everything at once, it is important to look at our schedules and the demands placed on us by others (and ourselves) honestly. For example, perhaps you may try and squeeze in a session with a client even though you don't really have time and the session ends up leaving you exhausted? Not only is it impossible to find a sense of inner calm when your attention is split in too many ways but there just isn't time to recover. While there are times when running on automatic pilot is beneficial, there are also times when it may hinder your health, well-being and professional performance.

Noticing when you're on autopilot

Mindfulness practice can help you begin to spot those moments when you react automatically. Noticing these moments is a prerequisite for change. While this initial awareness does not change anything in itself, it affords you the opportunity to choose what you're going to do next.

Transfer to the therapeutic context

In the therapeutic context the perception of such automatic reactions can serve a useful diagnostic function – for example, in order to comprehend what reactions the patient might experience and how these are to be understood in the context of the reasons they came to see you. At the same time, being aware of the impulse to react automatically, without actually doing so, provides the option to discuss such impulses with the client. You can explore this practically using the extension of the sitting meditation outlined below.

Exercise 13: Sitting meditation (with 'non-responsiveness', 15 minutes)

Sit in a relaxed, upright position. Follow your breath as it enters each of the three body regions (the nose, the upper chest/heart region and the abdomen). Starting with your inhalation, feel the cool air as it flows through your nose and see if you can follow it as it enters your lungs. Notice how your ribcage and abdomen rise with your breath. When you're ready to exhale, notice as your lower abdomen begins to fall and your chest follows. If you count your breaths as you exhale, try to let the counting take a back seat and focus more on your physical sensations. If you notice that your mind wanders, just be aware of that. Perhaps you are thinking of something that you are looking forward to or maybe your mind is lingering on a difficult topic. As you notice these impulses, remind yourself that right now all you need to do is follow your breath. Perhaps you notice that you want to change your posture. Try just sitting with that impulse for a minute or so and noticing what happens. Continue to do this for 15 minutes.

Reflect on this exercise for a moment. What did you notice? How easy was it for you to perceive the various stimuli and the evaluative thoughts? For example, perhaps you were thinking about an event that you were looking forward to and thought 'I don't want to go back to my breath, this is fun!' Or you might have noticed a slight tingling in your feet due to the position you were sitting in and thought 'this is so uncomfortable, why continue?' Or maybe something else?

Non-reacting in everyday life

Informal exercises can be used to work with the non-reacting element of mindfulness. By practising such exercises daily you can strengthen your ability to choose how to respond to situations rather than reacting to them automatically. Here are a few examples:

1. Your phone rings, how do you feel? Perhaps the impulse to run away? It seems that many therapists experience this regularly!
2. Perhaps a song you don't like comes on the radio. You can use this as an opportunity to notice that you don't like it but resist the automatic impulse to turn it off or change the station.
3. Next time you're at the supermarket checkout, observe how fast the other queues move forward. If other queues are moving faster just observe any thoughts or feelings that pop up. If you want to switch queues try just being aware of that impulse.
4. When you're watching television, notice how you feel when the adverts come on.

Now take a moment to think over situations in your everyday life, private and/or professional, where watching your everyday impulses may be helpful. Don't just think about situations where you regret your behaviour. Think about situations where you may no longer even be aware of these impulses anymore. For example, people in the helping professions may be a little too forgiving at times. Have you said to yourself 'he can't help it, he's behaving this way because of "X", I can't be angry'? By doing this our natural needs are dismissed and over time may no longer even be perceived. This, in turn, may lead to frustration and a loss of self-esteem, which may cause us to be less satisfied with our lives. Becoming aware of our natural reactions can be really helpful. You could check in with yourself after each session with a client or at the end of the day. You could try asking yourself questions such as 'Was I pushed beyond my limits – if so, how did I react?' Or you could ask yourself 'Have I tended to my needs today?' Most of us in the helping professions are focused on providing the best possible care for our clients, regardless of the cost to ourselves. This programme aims to remind you to show yourself the same respect and care you show your clients. Exercise 14 might be a helpful starting point. It is not intended to be used regularly but may be helpful if you are feeling particularly overwhelmed.

Exercise 14: Leaves on a river (10–15 minutes)

Think back to a situation where you were angry or insecure. What was happening? Who was involved? Did you have some responsibility for the situation? What thoughts did you have then? What thoughts pop up now when you reflect on that situation? What body sensations do you notice? How would you describe the most prominent feeling you associate with that situation? How would you rate that feeling on a scale of 0–100, with 100 being the most intense?

Now take a moment to imagine you are sitting on a river-bank and you realise you can place your upsetting thought or feeling on a leaf and watch it float away on the river. You can decide to release anything you like in this way – even people. If you feel that leaves are not sturdy enough to bear the weight of your issue you can imagine building a small raft for them. As your issue floats away down the river, you notice it becoming smaller and smaller on the horizon. Once all related situations, people, issues, thoughts and feelings, have floated into the distance, return to the present moment. How do you feel right now? How does your body feel? Do any thoughts pop up? Now think about the initial issue again and notice how intense it is on a scale of 0–100.

How did you find the exercise? Were you able to put all of the various aspects of your situation onto the leaves/rafts and let them drift away? Perhaps you found, like many of those who've attended this programme, that this exercise helped to decrease the intensity of the thoughts, feelings and body reactions associated with the issue you picked? If so, you have been able to take a step back from the situation and observe it from a different perspective.

Once in a while you may find that you don't have time for your regular sitting meditation. In such cases you might like to try the following short meditation.

Exercise 15: In a nutshell (1–3 minutes)

For this exercise observe your breath for 30 breaths, counting the exhalations. If you find you have lost track of where you are you can either start again from the last number you remember or start from scratch.

How was that? You can do this meditation almost anywhere and at any time.

Exercises for the week ahead

- Exercise 5: Flash mindfulness (three times daily).
- Mindfulness diary (daily).
- Exercise 13: Sitting meditation (daily, minimum 15 minutes).
- Experiment with the non-reacting exercises (at least three times in the week).
- Reflect on your own needs (daily).

Have fun practising!

3.5 Week 5: Mindfulness as a Home Base for Therapists

Begin this session by checking in with yourself. What thoughts are going through your mind? What physical sensations are you aware of? What emotions are you experiencing? What is your general health like? Just notice whatever presents itself without judgment.

Take a moment to look back over your mindfulness diary. What new experiences have you had? Are you satisfied with the frequency and duration of your practice? What would you like to do differently in the coming week?

Contents of the fifth week

In the first few weeks of MBHP we focused on bringing mindfulness into your private life. This week we will shift the focus slightly and concentrate more on how mindfulness can be useful in the workplace.

Mindfulness in the therapeutic context

As we begin this session, please take a moment to reflect on the following points. Try to be open, accepting and non-judgmental.

- How do you feel about being a therapist?
- How do you feel about your work, your colleagues, your clients?
- How can mindfulness help you to become more perceptive regarding your own needs?
- What impact does this kind of attention have on your health and your well-being?

69

- What influence does this have on your clients?
- How do you find this process of self reflection?

There are a number of points you could have considered. Here are a few we came up with:

Mindfulness encourages shared discovery and reduces egocentric thought and experience. Perhaps you noticed that you are better able to slip between the first-person and second-person perspective, allowing you to perceive your evaluations of your clients? Perhaps you also noticed that choosing to monitor your reactions without judgment allows you to see that not all of your hypotheses about yourself, or your clients, are necessarily absolute truths, but rather interpretations based on your knowledge and experience. The non-reacting aspect of mindfulness can also help you to look at your clients as they are, before turning your attention to how you may be able to help them.

Mindfulness can also help both the therapist and the client by helping to balance existing contradictions. It could be argued that there are four key contradictions in psychotherapy:

1. The client talks to you about private matters which he would usually only discuss with close friends or family, perhaps even paying for the service.
2. While you may have received thorough training in your field, this does not automatically mean that you are any more successful at managing your life and applying this knowledge practically than your client. Similarly, many of your clients may have a good understanding of how they could approach things differently, yet they do not put theory into practice. Despite the knowledge that they are 'only human', many therapists still have impossibly high standards and expect themselves to behave perfectly all of the time.

3. You may find yourself idealised on the one hand and regarded with suspicion on the other. For example, clients may think 'Oh, you're capable of unravelling all of my problems and providing an omnipotent solution', or something in that vein. In doing so they place you on an imaginary pedestal. Conversely, they may be suspicious and think 'I must be careful what I say; I don't want to be analysed and judged'.
4. There is both praise and blame in therapy. For example, clients may think that in your role as a therapist you are able to solve every problem or concern and may feel let down when they realise this is not the case. You may even buy into this a little yourself, perhaps feeling like a failure and wondering if all those years of training were really worth it. Or, you may feel frustrated with your clients, perhaps even blaming them for not participating fully.

These, seemingly paradoxical, conditions are commonplace and highlight some of the burdens on people in the helping professions. Bringing a mindful awareness to these contradictions can provide you with the space to consider how you want to respond to them. But for now, let's go back to the very beginning and explore how you greet your clients.

Greet the client

How do you normally greet your clients? Is the first step opening the door or calling for them to enter? Or does the process begin earlier? For example, do you get out the file and re-read the minutes of your last session again? Do you use any rituals to allow you to let go of your last client and focus on the next one? Don't rush this – make time to reflect on each of these points.

Now, perhaps you'd like to consider if you could manage this process more mindfully. We asked this to some of the participants who have attended these workshops face to face and they came up with the following points:

- Sometimes thoughts of your last client may linger as you greet, or prepare to greet, your next client. You could choose to use a variation of Exercise 14 (Leaves on a river).
- As you prepare to greet your client you might like to take a moment to check in with yourself and notice any spontaneous reactions you may have, without judgment, perhaps even naming them.
- You could try a short meditation like Exercise 15 (In a nutshell), or some variation, to bring yourself fully into the present moment.
- You could experiment by beginning your sessions with a brief joint mindfulness exercise.
- If you are feeling particularly drained, Exercise 16 (below) might be a useful way to reconnect with yourself.

Exercise 16: Tree meditation (15 minutes)

Find a relaxed, upright, standing position and observe your breath. Once you feel stable, with each exhalation imagine that your feet are growing roots into the ground. With each exhalation the roots become deeper, stronger, more stable. You might be able to almost 'see' or 'feel' this, but don't worry if not. When you feel that your roots are deep enough, move onto the next stage. With each inhalation, imagine you are absorbing nutrients from the earth. With each exhalation, imagine your 'roots' growing deeper and stronger into the ground. How do they feel? Are there several large roots or an array of smaller ones? As you continue this, feel yourself becoming more and more stable. When you're ready to bring this exercise to a close, spend a few moments just noticing how you feel.

This exercise doesn't fit easily into the usual break between clients of five to ten minutes. It's useful to practise this exercise for at least 15 minutes in the first instance, although it might take quite a bit longer to feel 'rooted' and stable. However, if you have practised regularly then you might find you are able to use this exercise usefully in shorter periods of time – possibly in just a few minutes. Because there are no clear-cut rules, we would like to invite you to try it out for yourself and see what works for you. There will be more body-orientated practices in Week 6.

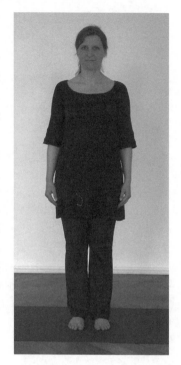

Exercise 17: Stabilising asanas

Take up a relaxed, upright posture (as in Exercise 16). Imagine your feet take root with the earth. To relieve your lower back muscles and to increase the security of the state, tense your pelvic muscles and rotate the knee outward slightly, while keeping your legs straight. (There might be no perceptible movement. The important thing is that you perceive the tension in the knees.) Raise your arms and elbows to heart level and place the hands in front of your chest with your palms pressed together lightly. Make sure you are standing straight and that your chest isn't tilted forward. As you inhale, imagine you are breathing in and out from your belly, if you can. Try and keep your shoulders relaxed and broad with your chin parallel to the ground. Then breathe in ten breaths in this position. You might even like to

think of a tree or a stable object, such as a tower or column, or even look at a picture of one. At the end of the exercise, take a few moments to notice any effects.

Standing with your legs a little more than hip-width apart, turn your left foot to the left so that it is pointing outwards. Your right foot remains pointing forwards. Your body should be facing forwards. You will need to adjust your stance according to your height and flexibility. Be gentle and take a moment to find a position that is comfortable. Raise your arms outstretched, parallel with your shoulders (again, if that is possible for you). Then turn your

head to the left and bend your left knee so that your left knee is in line with the toes of your left foot. Look out over your fingertips. Feel the power of that movement as you breathe calmly and evenly. When you're ready, gently come back to the centre and, standing straight, notice how you feel. Has anything changed? Then repeat the exercise on the right side. Again, come back to the centre when you're ready and check in with yourself. You might like to shake your arms and legs a little to finish the exercise.

Standing in your relaxed, upright position once again, raise your arms above your head and interlink your fingers. Contract the muscles of your core for stability and stretch your arms upwards as far as is as comfortable, breathing steadily. Depending on the mobility of your shoulders you might even like to try moving your arms slightly behind your head.

If you have any back problems, please be very cautious with the next part of the exercise and use your own common sense as to whether you should try this. On your next exhalation you might like to try bending forward slightly, keeping your back straight and

your arms above your head. Only go as far as is comfortable. With the next inhalation, move back to an upright standing position. Try this a couple of times. Finally, come back to the standing position and notice how you are now.

You could choose to use these exercises individually in gaps throughout your day, or you could try them in sequence. You could also try combining them with some of the other exercises. Feel free to experiment with these, and all of the exercises and find out what works best for you.

Exercise 18: 'There is ...' (5–10 minutes)

Once again, take up a relaxed upright position. Close your eyes and notice how you feel. What are your first thoughts? As you become aware of your thoughts, just say to yourself 'There is a thought ...' Do this for a little while until you have looked at all your current thoughts. Try to observe what is there without judging it. If you like, you could expand this to your body. You can begin from your feet or your head, whichever you prefer. You could also choose to start from the heart area and move outwards. Each time you notice something, such as an itchy nose or some tension in your calf, just name it (for example, 'there is some tension in my calf'). Once you feel you have noted all of your physical sensations, you might like to widen this exercise out to include your emotions. For every emotion you become aware of just say to yourself 'There is a feeling of ...' When you're ready, bring the exercise to a close.

How was that? Was anything particularly enjoyable or difficult? This exercise is a deeper version of our usual weekly 'check in', at the start of each week. It can also be used in a therapeutic context, to help you stay in tune with yourself and your client, and also to help you be aware of any automatic reactions you have to your client. We have found it useful to spend some time in each session with our clients, noting our own reactions, which in turn has helped us fully engage with our clients in an authentic way.

However, there can be difficulties with this approach. From our experience, and that of participants on our courses, we are aware that it can be difficult to pay attention to how you're reacting to your client while still remaining present with your client and listening to what they are saying. This is a skill that develops naturally over time, with practice. We suggest that you start by trying it out in the coming week during your private conversations. For example, your child might be telling you something about what happened at school, you could be discussing plans for the coming week with your partner, or even listening to a sales pitch on the telephone. During the conversation take note of how you feel. What thoughts have popped up? How is your body? Tense? Relaxed? Are you aware of any emotions? How do they relate to the conversation you're having? Do you want to change anything? For example, are you irritated by the sales pitch and want to cut the salesperson off? Or are you excited, realising you do need a new 'x' and this is a good price? After trying it out in your personal life, the next step will be to try to bring this awareness to your therapeutic sessions.

Exercises for the week ahead

- Exercise 5: Flash mindfulness (three times daily).
- Mindfulness diary (daily).
- Exercise 16: Tree meditation and/or Exercise 17: Stabalising asanas (daily).
- Experiment with bringing mindful awareness to the way you greet your clients.

- Check in with yourself during conversations in your private life. How are you? Name thoughts, feelings and sensations (daily).
- Exercise 13: Sitting meditation (daily, minimum 15 minutes).

Good luck!

3.6 Week 6: Mindfulness of the Body

As usual, we'll begin Session 6 by taking a moment to check in with ourselves. Take a moment to notice your body. What physical sensations are you aware of? What thoughts are going through your mind? How do you feel?

Now take a moment to think back over your meditation practice for the last week. It might be useful to look through your meditation diary. How has your practice been going? How do you feel about that? Do any particular thoughts arise? Were you able to integrate mindfulness into your work? How motivated do you feel to continue practising?

Contents of Week 6

This session will focus on body-oriented forms of meditation, such as those found in yoga. These exercises are divided into smaller sequences which are easy to incorporate into your working day.

Mindful movement

Mindful movement can be viewed as another way of meditating, which is a nice variation for some and welcome respite for others who find staying still for 20 minutes difficult. Mindful movement may lead to a deeper level of body awareness which, in turn, may serve to facilitate mindfulness on another level. After all, if one is not fully present and aware of one's own body, it is difficult to see how one can be fully present and aware of others.

It is no accident that yoga has formed part of the religious and cultural tradition in the East, and has been described as "The ability to focus exclusively on one subject, question or

79

any other content, and to linger in this direction without distraction" (Desikachar, 1999). This is the second verse from the 'Yoga Sutra' of Patanjali, an ancient yoga text, which highlights the strong meditative aspect of yoga. While there are many different types of yoga, this book will introduce you to a selection of basic movements. They are simple movements which we hope will help you to become more aware of your body and your breath.

As always, before attempting any of the movements please pay particular attention to your own personal limits. This is a key aspect of being fully present within your body and is necessary to ensure you are able to engage with the movements fully without exceeding your own limits. All kinds of things can influence your movements – your fitness level, the heat of the room, or even the time of day. For example, you might feel stiffness in the morning, but find you have a much greater range of movement in the evening. So it is particularly important to come to each movement with a fresh, accepting attitude and notice how it feels and how long it is comfortable to stay in the position.

The following exercises were put together to be used at any time, but are particularly suitable for the office.

We have divided the exercises into different sequences, so you can choose to do them all in sequence, if you like, or just pick the ones that appeal to you. If you do decide to complete all the exercises, please note that it is important for your muscles to stay warm. If you take a long pause between the movements and find you've cooled down, repeat Exercise 19 to warm up again. It is important to leave two or three hours after a big meal before beginning the sequences (about an hour after a snack). Please make sure you drink plenty of water before and during the session and take time to cool down at the end. Finally, please remember that pain is a signal to stop. Listen to your body!

Exercise 19: Easing back

Start by putting your hands together and rubbing them until they feel warm and the hand muscles are soft. In traditional Chinese medicine many areas of the hands relate to other areas of the body, hence warming and softening the hands may also affect other muscles in the body. You might then like to massage one hand with the thumb of your other hand and then swap over. Take a couple of minutes for this.

If you're standing, put your hands on the back of your thighs. Feel free to adapt this to ensure you don't over-stretch. If you're sitting, put your hands just above your knees on your thigh. For this exercise, the movement always begins in the coccyx and follows the line of your spine, vertebra by vertebra and finally

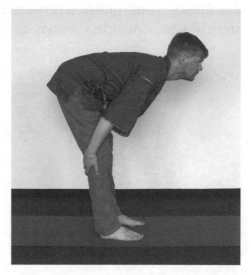

moving your neck last. Your arms should remain where they are throughout the movement. Gently hollow your back, starting at the coccyx, and then finally tilt your head upwards as you inhale. Then, as you exhale, slowly reverse the movement, again remembering to start at your coccyx, and arch your back up like a cat and let your head tilt downwards, following the line of your spine. Move in time with the natural rhythm of your breath. Repeat the entire sequence ten times.

You can try a variation of this at your desk. Sitting a short distance from your desk, with both feet firmly on the floor, put your hands on the desk in front of you. You can then arch and hollow your back gently in line with your breath.

You can use these exercises to relax your back, throat and neck muscles. They might help with things like tension headaches.

Exercise 20: Shoulder–neck area

You can do this exercise standing or sitting. Begin by lifting both your shoulders to your ears and then draw them backwards, so that there is a little pressure between the shoulder blades. Then stretch your shoulders down towards the ground before

bringing them back to the starting position. Please do this very gently and if you feel any resistance try doing the movement even more gently. Go at your own pace and really focus all your attention on the movement. Do this for about a minute at your own speed.

Now change direction and circle your shoulders forward. Again, take about a minute for this at your own speed.

Next, pull your shoulders up to your ears as you inhale and tilt your head towards your chest. Hold this position for a moment, then when you are ready, exhale and return your head and shoulders to the starting position. Pause for a moment and then repeat this exercise.

Now hold your head upright in a relaxed position and look straight ahead. Take a deep breath and raise your arms and clasp your hands behind your head with elbows pointing to the side. Turn your head to the left side, exhaling, without changing the position of the hands and elbows to the head. You should see your left elbow. Do not move the rest of the upper body. Only your head should be turned to the left. Then when you're ready to inhale, move your head slowly back to the centre. When you're ready to exhale, repeat the movement on the right side, rotating your head as far as is comfortable. Then as you inhale, return your head to the centre.

For the next movement, keep your head upright and look straight ahead. Your arms should be by your sides. Drop your head to the left shoulder, being careful not to strain. Only go as far as is comfortable. If you would like to intensify the stretch, you can bend your palm upwards, as illustrated, so the palm is parallel to the floor. Do this for about 30 seconds and move your head back to its original position. Then repeat on the right side. Again, this should take about 30 seconds.

Tilt your head forwards towards your chest for approximately 30 seconds.

Finally, imagine that your nose has a pen or a piece of chalk attached to it. With your nose, write your first and last name in the air (for this you don't need to worry about dotting the i's).

Exercise 21: Revival

The following exercises are best done standing. If you are unable to stand, you might like to adapt the exercise by sitting with your legs chair-width apart.

Standing tall, place your left hand on your waist and bend forwards until your torso is parallel with the floor. Let your

right arm hang loose. You might like to swing your right arm in front of your legs like a pendulum, if that is comfortable for you. This should be a very gentle, almost passive, motion. Exert as little force as possible to move your arm. Repeat this movement the other way around, that is, the right arm is at the waist, the left is the pendulum.

Standing straight again, raise both arms up so they are parallel to your ears with your fingers pointing towards the ceiling. Bend forwards as far as you can with your arms remaining beside your ears. Once you feel that you have reached as far as you can without straining, breathe deeply and try to move a little further forward as you aim your face towards your thighs and let your head, upper body and arms hang loosely for five breaths. Then, staying where you are, grasp whatever part of your body you can reach –

perhaps your knees, your calves or even your toes. Move your chin as close to your body as comfortably as you can. Breathe deeply in and out, about seven times. Then roll

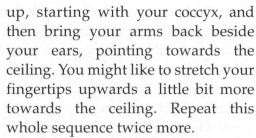

up, starting with your coccyx, and then bring your arms back beside your ears, pointing towards the ceiling. You might like to stretch your fingertips upwards a little bit more towards the ceiling. Repeat this whole sequence twice more.

Standing upright with your arms by your sides, push your shoulder blades together and clasp your hands behind your back, interlacing your fingers. Your palms should be facing one another. On your next inhalation, let your neck sit loosely and push your pelvis forwards and arch the upper part of your body backwards and push your chest forwards. Hold this position for five breaths. As you exhale, see if you can let go of

any tension in the shoulder muscles and move your shoulders a little bit further down and back. Then come to centre, keeping your hands interlaced behind you. When you're ready, slowly bend forwards. When you feel as though you have reached your full stretch you might like to lift your arms up behind your back as far as they will go. Hold this for about five breaths. As you exhale see if you can push a little further forwards. Then come back to centre and repeat the process again.

For this exercise, take an upright posture and stretch out however you like. Then breathe, with your mouth wide open, as though you were yawning. If the impulse to yawn comes, go with it. If it doesn't, you might like to play around making a yawn sound and see if it comes. Repeat this five times.

The activities in this Exercise 21 are often perceived as invigorating. As such, it is best to do them early in the day, or if you find yourself getting tired, in the afternoon.

Exercise 22: Reducing tension and anger

Begin by standing in an upright position with your hands up in the air by your ears with your fingertips pointing to the ceiling. Take five deep breaths in this position.

Then you can drop your arms beside your body and place your right hand on your left shoulder and your left hand on your right shoulder. Breathe deeply in and out five times and then release.

Let your arms fall to your sides and give your whole body a shake for at least a minute. Pay particular attention to your limbs. You might like to try and shake away any tension you notice in your body. As you do this you may find yourself thinking about people, events or feelings you

would like to 'shake'. Just notice what comes to mind and see what happens as you continue to shake your body. Once you've had enough, return to standing and place your arms out in front of you at shoulder height, open your eyes and mouth wide and let out a load roar! Repeat this process twice more.

Finally, return to a relaxed, upright posture. The following is a breathing sequence. As you inhale, count slowly from 1 to 4. Pause for a moment and hold the air in your body. You may like to try counting slowly from 1 to 8, or if that feels uncomfortable simply start exhaling when you're ready. As you exhale, count slowly from 1 to 4. Repeat this exercise two more times.

This sequence is particularly good if you're feeling tense, annoyed or a bit angry.

Exercise 23: Calming/relaxation

Start this exercise standing upright with your palms pressed together in front of your chest. Inhale and exhale seven times, focusing your breathing rhythm on the area where your palms meet. Then stretch your arms, with the palms still touching, upwards towards the ceiling. Your arms should be roughly parallel with your ears. As you breathe in, stretch upwards and push your fingertips closer to the ceiling. As you breathe out, relax your arms and, still keeping your palms together, drop your hands so they are just above your head. Repeat this cycle seven times. Move at your own pace and follow your own breathing rhythm.

Now we will try some yoga for your face! Start standing upright with your feet on the floor and your hands by your sides. As you inhale, tense your facial muscles and see if you can push them towards your nose. It might help to imagine you've just bitten into a lemon! As you exhale, look towards the ceiling with your eyes and mouth wide open and let out a sigh. Repeat this sequence

twice more in your own time. You might feel a little silly at first, but why not give it a go?

Next, rub your hands together quickly so you generate some heat in your palms. Then close your eyes and place your palms over your eyes with your palms resting on your cheekbones and your fingertips on your forehead. Take five breaths or so with your palms in this position. Then open your eyes.

You might like to do this next segment at an open window. Breathe in and out through your nose. Just go at your own pace, don't try and influence the speed of your breath, just watch as it rolls in and out, a bit like waves on the shore. When you're ready, breathe in deeply for about seven breaths, letting your breath fill your lungs and imagining your breath is going all the way to your stomach. It might help to put one or both hands on your stomach so you can actually feel the movement. Then shift your attention to your lower rib area and take another seven breaths. With each inhalation notice how the rib area expands in all directions before withdrawing as you exhale. It might help for you to put your hands flat on either side of your ribcage so you can feel the movement. Then bring your focus to the upper part of your chest and collarbone. As you take another seven breaths notice the natural rise and fall in that area, perhaps placing a hand on your sternum if you want to.

The final breathing sequence puts all three of these together. As you inhale, feel the air move to the lower stomach area and notice the abdominal wall lift up, then notice as your breath expands your lower ribs and then finally, as it fills your upper chest and that area lifts. As you exhale, exhale from your stomach first, then your lower rib area, and then finally from your upper chest. Do this seven times at your own pace. When you have finished take a few moments to breathe normally and notice how your body feels.

These exercises are quite calming so they are excellent to practise at the end of the day to relax, or if you've had to deal with a stressful situation.

Exercises for the week ahead

- Exercise 5: Flash mindfulness (three times daily).
- Mindfulness diary (daily).
- Practise one of the mindful movement sequences (Exercises 19–23) daily. If you do not want to practise mindful movement, please practise Exercise 13 (daily, minimum 15 minutes).

We hope you enjoy experimenting with mindful movement!

References

Desikachar, T. K. V. (1999). *The heart of yoga: Developing a personal practice*. Rochester, VT: Inner Traditions International.

Johnson, W. (2000). *Aligned, relaxed, resilient: The physical foundations of mindfulness*. Boston, MA: Shambhala.

3.7 Week 7: Integrating Mindfulness into Therapeutic Practice

Take a moment to reflect: Do you notice any particular sensations in your body? What thoughts are going through your mind? How do you feel? How is your general health? Take some time to check in with yourself and notice what is there.

Have a look at your diary from the last week. How did you get on with the yoga exercises? Has that had any impact on your practice this week? How motivated do you feel to continue establishing your mindfulness practice? Why do you think that is?

Contents of the seventh week

Week 7 will help you strengthen your mindfulness practice and look at more ways you can integrate mindfulness into your workplace.

Draining clients

You might get a great deal of personal satisfaction from helping others and seeing them progress. However, alongside that satisfaction you may also experience difficulties in communicating with your clients, stress, bitterness and even a sense of failure, regardless of your good intentions. In some ways this can be viewed as a fundamental part of working with others, but it can become an issue when stress and worry, relating to a particular client, impacts your work with others and perhaps even spills over into your personal life. Perhaps you can think of a current client you find challenging in this way? If not, perhaps someone from the past? Use one such contact for the next exercise.

Exercise 24: Picture and release (about 5 minutes)

For this exercise take a relaxed, upright position. Begin by observing your breathing for about three minutes. Then, when you are ready, recall the client you were just thinking about. As you bring that client to mind notice your body – is there any change? What thoughts or emotions come to mind? Name them and then let them go while you return your focus to your breathing. If they come back, let them be there, and then return your focus to your breathing. When it feels right, bring that client back to mind. What do you notice this time? Is the image or feeling of the client the same or different? When you're ready, return your attention to your breathing for another minute, to close.

What effect did the exercise have on you? Note whatever comes to mind, no matter what it is. Even if you feel as if it didn't have any effect. Just accept whatever presents itself to you. This informal mindfulness practice is an opportunity to practise observing what comes to mind, rather than assessing it.

Some people experience a bit more distance between themselves and their client the first time they do this exercise. For others it takes more time. Repeat this exercise several times until you feel there is enough distance between you and your client that your associated reactions have decreased. You may wish to repeat this exercise immediately – it is up to you.

Mindful listening

Mindful listening involves more than paying close attention to what is said by another. It also involves being aware of the automatic reactions you may have to what is said and the assumptions you make. For example, if a challenging client usually reacts in a certain way, it is easy to respond automatically to what you expect, rather than what actually happens. Further, mindfulness can help us be aware of how we are experiencing the interaction. For example, it is useful to be aware if you are finding it difficult to remain focused on the conversation – and why. It is also helpful to consider any conclusions you've already made and what has informed them. Are they based on your practical experience, academic knowledge, intuition, personal beliefs, or some combination of these?

Mindful listening creates an inner stillness in which your client may appear free of your preconceptions and prejudices.

Exercise 25: Mindful listening

If you have a partner to help with this exercise, ask them to talk for five to ten minutes about something fairly neutral, such as what they did at the weekend or the last movie they saw. For this exercise, you are aiming to be a sounding board for your partner. Keep eye contact but don't engage in conversation beyond a few comments or nods in line with what is being said. Simply listen. While your partner is speaking, be aware of your body and your breath. How is your posture? What comes to mind as you listen to your partner? Are you judging or evaluating what is being said? Name any judgments or evaluations and then let go of them. The aim is to be fully present and listening to your partner.

If no partner is available at the moment, turn on the radio or TV and listen to something in the same manner.

If you practised with another person, discuss the exercise. Did your partner feel listened to? Share your own experience, too. Try and remember some key elements of the conversation and check that you heard the information correctly. If you didn't have a partner, reflect on your own experience and try to recall what you were listening to. If you did this exercise alone you might like to try it with a partner in the future so you can compare the experience.

Extension of the exercise: You can do this again, but this time let your mind wander. How is this different? If you did this exercise with a partner, discuss your experiences.

Many participants on our courses worried that they would miss a lot of information when they did the mindful listening exercise as they were focusing on their own body, breath and thoughts. While this wasn't generally the case (see also Exercise 17), it does seem that more details are remembered the more one practises. The narrator also reported giving a more detailed account and feeling more motivated to continue telling the story when the other person was listening mindfully.

Burnout

The previous exercise touched upon how stressful interacting with others may be. As discussed in Chapter 2, those in the helping professions are at a particular risk of experiencing burnout. It is common for individuals to set themselves high personal standards over and above professional requirements. Perhaps you have noticed one or more of the following. Have you been dissatisfied at the end of a working day when you were not able to offer an immediate solution to a tricky situation? Or perhaps you felt the tension between the client-focused aspects of your work and the associated paperwork. Maybe you found that you were really tired and needed more rest, but didn't feel able to take time for yourself. Or did you feel that you were not progressing quickly enough in your career and pressured yourself to do more training, publish more or take on additional management responsibilities? It is easy to keep stacking pressure after pressure upon yourself, which, in conjunction with the frequent lack of objective measures of performance, can lead to burnout if unaddressed. Exercise 26 is a mindfulness exercise that can help you become more aware of the demands you place on yourself and to look at them with fresh eyes. It also prompts you to consider what good performance means to you.

Exercise 26: Heart meditation (10–15 minutes)

Take a relaxed, upright posture and close your eyes. Move your focus throughout your body for a few moments. If you notice any tension, try to release it. Place your hand on your sternum, over your heart. Focus on this area and notice as your hand moves in line with your breath. As you breathe, remember your body needs oxygen to live and that your heart is distributing oxygen around your body. As you breathe you might like to imagine that you're breathing directly in and out of your heart. If you don't want to do that, just keep focusing on the area as you continue breathing. Do this for three to five minutes. You can leave your hand where it is or move it down beside you or on to your lap.

Now, if it feels right for you, you might like to become aware of aspects of your life you might be finding difficult or stressful. Name any mental, physical or emotional reactions. Gently notice what is there. If you find you are judging yourself or others, look at it and then let go of those thoughts and feelings. There is no need to rush. You have plenty of time. Let any thoughts, feelings, images or concepts emerge regarding your life and any pressures you're experiencing. Let them be there for a moment, then, when you exhale, let them go. It's OK if the same issue or concept keeps coming to your mind – you're not doing anything wrong. Let whatever it is be there for a moment and take a look at it as gently as possible and then choose to let it go. Remind yourself that your focus is in the present moment and there is nothing else you need to pay attention to right now. Remember too that you are enough, irrespective of your current status or any issues you experience. Every time thoughts pop into your head, raising issues or judgment, name them and smile a little to yourself. If you like, you can come up with a simple phrase that embodies this friendly support.

Put your hand back on your sternum, over your heart, and say this phrase to yourself, mentally, for the next three to five minutes. You might like to imagine you take these words into your heart. When you finish this exercise take a few moments to stop and reflect. How was it?

Exercises for the week ahead

- Exercise 5: Flash mindfulness (three times daily).
- Mindfulness diary (daily).
- Listen mindfully in personal interactions (daily).
- Exercise 13: Sitting meditation (daily, minimum 15 minutes), followed by Exercise 26: Heart meditation (minimum ten minutes).

Good luck with your practice!

3.8 Week 8: Review and Next Steps

As we begin this final week, stop for a moment and reflect: How do you feel about this being the last session? What thoughts are you aware of? How does your body feel? Something else?

Contents of Week 8

This final session aims to consolidate everything we've covered and to provide some inspiration as you go forward and establish your mindfulness practice.

Review

Begin by reflecting on how you've found the various mindfulness practices. Take your time with this. Which suit you best? Do you feel as though you have established a regular practice? Why? How do you feel about that? What has motivated you to practise? Have you noticed any moments when mindfulness has 'leaked' into your life? Perhaps you normally get angry in a traffic jam but you were able to relax and let go? Or maybe you noticed that when a client frustrated you, you were able to leave that in the office, rather than taking it home with you? Despite the benefits, establishing a solid mindfulness practice is not easy, and requires a deep personal commitment.

Considering your personal experience and the evidence presented in this book, how do you think it could benefit you in the future?

Before moving on to consider how you can take your practice forward, we'll do a walking meditation.

Exercise 27: Mindful walking

Stand in a relaxed, upright position with your feet close together. Lift one foot up as you inhale and move it forward. As you exhale, keep moving the foot forward to complete the

98

step and place the foot down on the ground in front of you. With your next inhalation lift the back foot slightly and start moving it forward. Around the midway point exhale as you complete the step forward. Breathe naturally and let your movement follow your breath. Your focus should be on the movement of each foot – paying particular attention to the way the foot feels as it lifts off the ground, 'floats' forward, and makes contact with the ground. You can either leave your hands hanging loosely by your side or you can intertwine your hands in front of you. Your gaze should be slightly lowered to the ground a few feet in front of you. As you do this exercise, notice if you feel the impulse to speed up or slow down. You might feel frustrated or wonder if you're doing it right. As ever, just notice what presents itself to you, gently, without judging it. Let those thoughts, feelings or impulses go, and return your attention to your walking. Do this for about 15 minutes.

Looking forward

It is useful to take some time to reflect on what has worked particularly well for you and to build a plan of how you wish to establish your mindfulness practice beyond this programme. You might like to consider the following points. Again, leave plenty of time for this!

- What is the best time of day for you to practise?
- Which formal mindfulness practices suit you best?
    - How long do you do them for?
    - Do you want to extend this over time?
- How frequently are you doing a formal meditation?
    - How do you feel about that?
        - What supports your practice?
        - What obstacles have you noticed to your practice?

99

- ° Would you like to increase this?
  - Why?
  - How can you do that?
- How will you reflect on your practice in the future?
  - ° Do you plan to continue using the mindfulness diary?
    - Do you want to adapt it?
    - How often will you use it?
    - Why?
  - ° Would it help to meet with colleagues to discuss your practice?
    - If so, would you rather meet in a group or one to one?

Note: From our experience, it is useful, at least at first, to take the time to reflect on your practice (alone or with others) fairly regularly. It is in the early days of your practice that you are most likely to find yourself saying you 'don't have time', 'will do it later on in the week', and so forth. Recognising this early can help you overcome it.

- How are you currently bringing the various techniques, such as attentive listening, into your working life?
  - ° How do you feel about that?
  - ° What other techniques would you like to build into your work?
    - How can you do that?
- Are you getting enough breaks in your day? Can you change something?

It is useful to make at least a rough outline, in writing, as soon as possible. This will help you reflect more deeply on how you can bring your mindfulness practice into your daily life. Specifically, it allows you to reflect on what you want to be doing now and how you might like to develop in the near future. It is also useful to plan regular time for longer, deeper meditations. See Section 3.9 for more details on this. You might also find it helpful to network with others and plan to practise together.

Successful failure

Over the last eight weeks we have practised various mindfulness exercises and you have probably, at times, found yourself frustrated because your mind has wandered and you haven't managed to stay focused. It is easy to become discouraged when we can't do something 'right' or achieve perfect mastery. However, such perfect mastery entails the perfect, everlasting attention to the present moment. That is impossible. If you move forward seeking this you will surely be disappointed, as those 'aha, I've done it' moments are followed by moments of carelessness.

This can be a frustrating experience. But must it be frustrating? What does it mean to be mindful 'successfully'? Let us consider the aims of mindfulness practice:

1. the intention to experience conscious focus on the present moment
2. to notice when your attention has accidentally 'wandered'
3. the smooth return of the attention to the present moment.

A certain amount of concentration and the ability to focus is of course helpful. But the ultimate goal is to keep our attention on the present moment. While we may pursue this, we are also aware that this can never be achieved. This is the 'successful failure' of mindfulness. Be gentle with yourself and focus on exercises that are easy for you as you establish a routine.

Final sitting meditation

Sit for about 15 minutes (see Exercise 11). When you finish, bring to your mind the question of what mindfulness practice means to you personally. Hold it gently and try not to be judgmental. Just notice what comes up over the next five minutes.

Congratulations! We wish you much joy as you continue to develop your mindfulness practice.

and see if some distance makes a difference. You might like to try cutting the apple to see if that makes a difference. Explore the apple carefully and decide where you are going to make the first cut. Why choose there? As you are ready to cut the apple, take a moment to notice your own posture and to feel the knife in your hand. As you prepare to cut the apple, notice the angle of the blade and feel the pressure as you make the first cut. You might like to close your eyes again and see if the smell of the apple has changed. Observe any other changes in your body, such as your mouth watering. Open your eyes and carefully finish cutting the apple. When you're ready, take a piece of apple and place it in your hand. What do you see? What do you see now that was hidden before the apple was cut? Bring the apple to your lips. What do you perceive? When you're ready, take a small bite and let it sit on your tongue. How is that? Does the taste change? You might like to move the apple around your mouth a little and be aware of how that is. If you notice the impulse to bite down, just notice that for a moment before acting on it. Then, bite down and be aware of the changing sensations, tastes and textures as you chew. Swallow the apple when you're ready. How was that? You can adapt this exercise for other foods.

Exercise 29: Keeping pace with the breath

Choose a place where you can take a stroll without being interrupted. You could do this somewhere scenic, like a beach or park, or even in your own garden or street. Start by walking at your natural pace for about two minutes. Then watch your steps for a minute or so, counting them as you go. From there, notice the natural rhythm of your breath and see if you can recognise how many steps you take per inhalation and exhalation. Do this for at least a minute. You can experiment with the length of each inhalation and exhalation and notice how that alters the number of steps you take per breath. Play with this for at least five minutes. Finally, shift your attention from your footsteps and your breathing to your surroundings. What do you see? What can you hear? How is the temperature? Do this for a minute or two and then finish the exercise.

Variants of sitting meditation

In the same way that you make your breath the anchor of your attention in the sitting meditation, you can choose to bring this awareness to an object. Once you have chosen your object, observe it non-judgmentally. What do you see? What thoughts, feelings or emotions pop up? Do you have a physical reaction to the object? Notice whatever presents itself then let go and bring your attention back to the object.

You might like to try this with a candle. Place the candle on a stool or low table about three feet away so you are looking slightly down and in front of yourself when you focus on the flame. As you look at the flame, try not to blink. You may find that you want to blink much more than usual – at least partly because you're trying not to! During this exercise it is normal that your eyes may fill with tears. Notice as this happens, along with your impulse to wipe away your tears or close your eyes. If your eyes start to burn, just close them for a few moments and notice how your eyes react. Maybe you see an after-image of the flame, bright spots or something else. Perhaps you notice a feeling of relief that you closed your eyes. Just notice what is there. When you're ready, open your eyes and focus on the flame once more. Do this meditation for at least ten minutes.

Another variation of the sitting meditation is to bring an image or concept, such as joy or calmness, to mind. As you sit you can focus on this concept, remembering to remain patient with yourself if you find your mind wanders. If you wish to include this exercise in your daily practice, it may be useful to stay with one image or concept, rather than picking new subjects daily or weekly.

An example

If you start your mindful oasis in the morning, you might like to go to your garden or balcony and do a five to ten minute breathing exercise (such as Exercise 23). If you decide to take a shower or bath, take the time to feel the water on your skin, or to notice the smell and texture of any soap or shampoo. You can choose whatever you like to focus on but it might be helpful to focus on one thing at a time. When you have your first drink of the day, drink it mindfully, bringing all your attention to it. Depending on how you feel, you might like to start off with an activating movement exercise (such as Exercise 10), or you may prefer a sitting meditation (minimum 15 minutes). When you're ready for breakfast, remember to eat at least some of it mindfully (see Exercise 28). As the day progresses you might like to try a walking meditation (Exercise 29). To close your session you might like to do a formal meditation such as the sitting meditation (Exercise 11).

The ideas presented in this section are intended as a starting point. They come from discussions at various mindfulness courses we have held over the last few years. Play with it!

107

4

Extending Your Practice

4.1 Going Deeper

The four foundations of mindfulness

This chapter will present the four principles of mindfulness, as outlined by Nyanaponika, a German Buddhist monk who spent many years in Sri Lanka. Nyanaponika's book, *Mind training through mindfulness* (1989) was first published in 1969 and is based on translations of larger discourses by the Buddha. (You don't have to be Buddhist to benefit from his understanding of mindfulness and its applications.) Each of the four principles of mindfulness will be explained alongside practical hints to help you deepen your practice.

Mindfulness for Therapists: Understanding Mindfulness for Professional Effectiveness and Personal Well-Being, First Edition. Gerhard Zarbock, Siobhan Lynch, Axel Ammann and Silka Ringer.
© 2015 John Wiley & Sons, Ltd. Published 2015 by John Wiley & Sons, Ltd.
Companion Website: www.wiley.com/go/zarbock/mindfulnessfortherapists

Mindfulness of the body
The first foundation of mindfulness is mindfulness of the body. The body is an ideal base for awareness training as it is always present in the here and now. There are many ways to develop mindfulness of the body. You can focus on the breath, noting each inhalation and exhalation, paying close attention to your posture and position, or focusing on more subtle physical sensations.

We introduced mindfulness of the breath and the breathing space in Chapter 3. Another great way to practise mindfulness is the body flash. Whenever you remember, take a short pause to check in with your body How does it feel?

You might also like to use small everyday actions such as unlocking doors, turning door knobs or climbing the stairs as triggers to practise mindfulness. Generally, we are not aware of our bodies during our daily activities. Think of how many times you turn a door knob. What if each time you did that you did it mindfully? You can get really creative with this.

Mindfulness of feelings ('vedana')
The second foundation of mindfulness is vedana, or mindfulness of feelings. In Pali, 'vedana' does not denote our emotions, but can be understood as the sequence of perceptual processing where stimuli are classified as pleasant, unpleasant or neutral.

This is understandable from an evolutionary biological perspective. When early humans became aware of a new stimulus, the first step was to evaluate it and determine whether it was a sign of danger, something positive, or something neutral. The ability to do this was not only useful, but essential. Our survival depended upon it.

Mindfulness of feelings involves bringing awareness to these automatic reactions and taking a closer look. Paying attention to these early evaluations requires two things. First, a conscious perception of the early stages of the processing process – the moment in which the stimulus is only just becoming conscious, as it emerges from the unconscious and automatic information processing. Second, you must become aware of the perception and label it as pleasant, unpleasant or neutral. During this process you are practising mindfulness by becoming aware of the perception, observing it and then naming it. Applying these three processes promotes non-reacting, as they slow down the otherwise automatic linking between stimuli and labels and responses. This deceleration allows for greater clarity. Greater clarity allows you to consider the long- and short-term consequences of any actions. In turn, this can lead to a reduction in suffering and increased compassion. Mindfulness of feeling, and the greater clarity associated with it, can lead to a reduction in habits and behaviours that lead to, or intensify, suffering. This helps you recognise that we all experience automatic reactions continuously, but they are not stable; and just because your initial reaction to something is unpleasant, it does not mean that it really is unpleasant. This metacognitive insight is incredibly helpful and can help you choose how you wish to respond, rather than react automatically. We don't usually become aware of our early perceptions and stimulus processing. Generally, a stimulus must be particularly intense before we become conscious of it. Hence, as we begin, we tend to become aware of thoughts and feelings such as anger, passion or greed first.

Try the following for about a week during your sitting meditation (for at least 20 minutes). As you sit, observe whatever thoughts, feelings or sensations may materialise. Are they pleasant, unpleasant or neutral? As you continue to sit, notice if these evaluations change over time. Perhaps a thought or sensation becomes unpleasant? Or maybe as you sit and take an open and friendly attitude to your experience, you notice something unpleasant starting to dissolve?

After you've practised this for a week, you might like to try it with another sense, such as hearing. You could try this during your formal meditation, or even when you have a quiet moment, perhaps while you're in a café. Close your eyes and notice what you hear. Notice whether you label the sounds as pleasant, unpleasant or neutral, and how that impacts you. Sounds of voices can easily trigger memories, associations, impulses and images. When you notice you've become distracted, simply 'let go' of those distractions and return your attention to what you can hear and notice whether you label sounds as pleasant, unpleasant or neutral.

As a further step, we invite you to accept the challenge to try this when you are out and about in a social situation. Next time you're sitting in a car or standing in a queue at the supermarket, notice whether you label situations, items or people as pleasant, unpleasant or neutral. Notice what this means to you. Take care not to spiral into 'chains of association', but rather keep your evaluations in the present. The aim of this exercise is to sensitise us to our early evaluation processes – the headlights of our consciousness.

Mindfulness of the mind

What Nyanaponika describes as a mental examination, we might describe as moods. While emotions can come and go abruptly, moods tend to have a longer duration of anywhere from ten minutes to hours, days or even weeks. Colloquially, one might also consider moods as coloured glasses through which we view the world. When we fall in love we tend to see everything through rose tinted glasses. A bill is due? Never mind, it can be sorted out. You've just had an argument with your colleague? Don't worry, it will blow over. Conversely,

I'm sure you're familiar with the grey days where everything seems to have a cloud hanging over it. Depending on our mood we may take a different perspective on situations and events. A good example of that is having a hangover. Due to excessive alcohol consumption and possibly also a lack of sleep the next day, you may be irritable, sensitive to light and experience mild motor co-ordination difficulties or problems concentrating.

The aim of this exercise is to help you to perceive your thoughts, feelings and reactions whilst also getting a sense of how they may colour your life. What 'glasses' are you wearing and how does that influence what you experience? While it is common to speak of being in a 'good' or 'bad' mood, it is possible to examine this more deeply and learn to understand yourself better. You might like to try categorising your own mood retroactively at the end of day. What emotions and thoughts accompanied you throughout your day (anger, success, holidays, happiness, 'not being good enough')? Try it out for a week or so.

Mindfulness of mental objects (emotions and thoughts)
Nyanaponika describes the fourth foundation of mindfulness as the contemplation of mental objects. In psychology we would speak of perception or thoughts. We will use the term emotion to refer to basic emotions like fear, anger, sadness, disgust, contempt, joy or happiness. These emotions are called basic because they are expressed across cultures. Despite some subtle nuances they share core features which are expressed facially. The so-called 'social emotions', such as pride, envy, jealousy and compassion, do not appear to be genetically pre-determined in the same way as the basic emotions appear to be. Modern evolutionary biology and psychology have demonstrated that emotions and cognition play important

roles in human coping mechanisms and adaptive processes. Emotions enable the rapid assessment of the environment and motivate behaviour, while cognitions provide a way of processing and storing that information. Only by cognitions is it possible for an individual to align one's own behaviour with long-term goals, cultural norms and rules. Cognition allows for verbal communication and the ability to share information quickly, which is particularly useful in our ever-changing landscape (LeDoux, 2004).

Emotions and emotional intelligence are often considered as important as traditional, cognitive intelligence (Goleman, 1995). Given the impact of emotions on our evaluations of ourselves, others and our environment, and the fact that these evaluations can motivate or demotivate us, it is useful to practise becoming more mindful of them. Emotions are often seen as 'background noise' to our daily lives and are usually only noticed if they are particularly intense. Mindfulness practice can help you to become more aware of less pronounced emotions. Whether we are aware of it or not, these subtle emotions have a large effect on our mood, thoughts, feelings and behaviour. A key first step is to become aware of your emotions then watch them, naming them as you go. The key basic and social emotions are listed in Table 4.1. It is useful to remember that emotions are designed to impact us quickly to help us to take prompt action. So the body reacts automatically. For example, depending on the emotion, your heart-rate may increase, blood pressure might change or noradrenaline may be released.

Since we usually assume that we are in complete control of our emotions, it is particularly powerful to begin to tune in to subtle emotions that we may not have been aware of, and to acknowledge that they can have a powerful influence on us. When we are exploring our emotions mindfully it is important

Table 4.1

Emotion	Triggering social situation	Tendency to act
Joy	I obtain or achieve something positive. A need or wish is being gratified.	Pleasure and relaxation or repetition or continuation of the successful act to increase the frequency of positive states.
Surprise	Something unexpected happens.	Cessation and inhibition of the habitual process of acting and in-depth exploration.
Guilt	I have transgressed a moral command or rule.	Reparation with the aim of renewed connecting with the social group.
Shame	I fall short of ideals, wishes and expectations regarding myself.	Hide and self-diminish in order to avoid criticisms from others.
Envy and jealousy	Somebody has got something (envy) or someone (jealousy) I don't have.	Taking away or destruction of the object or relationship with the aim of self-supply.
Compassion	Someone I feel connected with suffers.	Console and express understanding, possibly help actively.

to remember that emotions are closely interwoven with cognitions and evaluations. When an emotion occurs, it is not the event or situation itself,which triggers the emotion. Rather, it is the individual's assessment of it. The next step is to assess whether the appraisal is reasonable. A classic example of this would be the intense fear that might be felt if one was walking along a dusty road at dusk and saw a seemingly dangerous snake on the road. After a second look, which reveals that it isn't actually a snake, the fear is gone even though one may still feel 'shaken' for some time. It is important to keep in mind that you may experience more than one emotion at the same time, or may experience different emotions in quick succession. For example, imagine you're riding on the underground. An angry passenger puts his dirty feet up on the seat beside you, marking your clothes. You might feel angry at this, but as you look at the other passenger this might turn to fear as you think he looks very threatening and you become concerned for your safety. Through mindfulness we can often discover that behind anger lies another reaction, perhaps a sense of shame for getting angry, or an attempt to avoid feeling afraid. Mindfulness can help by observing such emotions without judgment, perhaps for the first time.

You might like to take a day to work on developing your awareness of your emotions. You could do one day per week or less frequently, as you prefer. Pick an emotion to work with for the whole day. This will make it easier to tune into your more subtle emotions. We suggest you begin with anger and resolve to be aware of all anger reactions and to note them down. At the end of the day you can look back and reflect on how many times you named anger and when you felt angry. We suggest you choose a positive emotion, such as joy, for the next day you work with your emotions. If tuning into your emotions in this way feels useful for you, you might like to work your way through the emotions listed in Table 4.1.

Mindfulness of thoughts

Mindfulness is often discussed alongside the concept of automatic thoughts (Beck, Rush, Shaw, & Emery, 1993). It is thought that automatic thoughts are triggered by events and interactions. For example, if you are at a party and you immediately think 'I'm out of place', or if you start a new job and find yourself thinking 'I can't do this' or 'I'm going to make a fool of myself', mindfulness training can help you to notice what is there and endeavour not to evaluate those thoughts or feelings. So if you find yourself thinking 'It's terrible that I have these negative thoughts', try to let go of that! Also, try to take a non-reacting approach. For example, don't ask yourself, 'Why am I having these thoughts, where do they come from'? or, 'It's the same idea that my mother has about it', in the context of mindfulness training, just notice what is there, name it and watch it, letting it go when you're ready. The Zen Buddhist teacher Thích Nhất Hạnh recommends adding a half smile as you observe your thoughts. This helps foster an attitude of gentleness and compassion towards yourself.

The following questions may be helpful when considering your work generally, or in relation to a specific client:

- What automatic thoughts pop up on Monday morning as you make your way to work?
- What automatic thoughts do you have when you have paperwork, such as insurance forms or reports, to complete?
- What automatic thoughts come to mind when you're due to meet with a client?
- What automatic thoughts do you have when you leave work at night?

You may notice amongst the variety of thoughts you have that there is a current 'hot topic'. Perhaps this is an upcoming meeting with a difficult client, or an upcoming holiday. Such topics lurk in the background of your daily activities and can influence your day. Notice when this 'hot topic' presents itself and let it be there for a moment, name it (e.g. 'head talk', 'patient anxiety' or 'vacation excitement/stress'), and when you're ready, let it go. Remember, even if your mind keeps returning to the topic, it doesn't mean you're doing it wrong. Just keep noticing it, letting it be there, naming it, and then letting it go. If a particularly pressing problem presents itself, you can write it down and set it apart with the intention of addressing it shortly. Mindfulness practice can help us to let tomorrow provide for itself. If we follow the advice of Thích Nhất Hạnh, we might also greet our concerns with a smile, rather than as condemnation.

References

Beck, A. T., Rush, A. J., Shaw, B. E., & Emery, G. (1993). *Kognitive Therapie der Depression (3. Aufl.)*. Weinheim: Beltz.

Bohus, M. (2002). *Borderline-Störung. Fortschritte der Psychotherapie*. Göttingen: Hogrefe.

Goleman, D. (1995). *Emotional intelligence*. New York: Bantam Books.

Grawe, K. (2004). *Neuropsychotherapie*. Göttingen: Hogrefe.

Ledoux, J. (2004). *Das Netz der Gefühle (3. Aufl.)*. Munich: dtv.

Nyanaponika, M. (1989). *Geistestraining durch Achtsamkeit*. Konstanz: Christiani.

Zarbock, G. (2008). *Praxisbuch Verhaltenstherapie*. Lengerich: Pabst.

4.2 Exercises in Everyday Personal and Professional Lives

As you go about your daily activities you are probably on autopilot much of the time. If you are able to catch yourself when you're running on autopilot, you are likely to find yourself 'lost', thinking about past or future events. Why is this so? In life it is often useful to examine past actions or events in order to try to understand why things happened, in order to learn from the experience and perhaps to attribute blame. It is of course important to think ahead, but focusing on the future may also result in feelings of fear and uncertainty as the future is never fixed. However, the present moment, which is the only time which is readily accessible to us, often rushes past without us even noticing it. Most people have experienced moments of contentment and peace when they feel they are really present. Often such moments are all too fleeting and are relegated to holidays or weekends, when people feel they have time to stop. It doesn't take a week in the Bahamas or an elaborate Sunday brunch to experience such moments. They can be found whenever you awaken to the present moment. Whether it is the ray of sunshine that lands on your desk as you wait for your computer to start, the chirping of the birds outside your window in the early morning or the first sip of your cup of tea, those moments can be found almost any time you focus on the present moment. If we always expect things to be perfect tomorrow then we can never be fully satisfied in the present. While this might be motivated by a sense of hope, focusing too much on the future can rob us of the beauty of now. We may find, having arrived at the 'destination', we may not be as happy as we expected to be. We may experience regret when we reflect on all the hours, days or even years of false fantasies we engaged in at the expense of living in the present moment.

119

Informal mindfulness exercises

In addition to the formal meditation practices, informal mindfulness practices can help you bring this mindful awareness into your life and remind you to stay in the present. You might like to think of these as mindfulness anchors, which you can imbed into your day.

4.2.1 Informal mindfulness exercises and experiments as an aid to the experience of the present
Here is an example of how one can transform something as simple as the daily commute into a mindfulness exercise. We've given a comprehensive 'current awareness report' from one of the authors in the hope of inspiring you to experiment with this yourself.

> I actually have a very pleasant route to work and usually go by bike. My ride leads me through many streets with Art Nouveau buildings, halfway around a lake and then along to my place of work. I've noticed that I often make this journey automatically, so I decided to use it as an opportunity to practise mindfulness. The following example comes from a day in early November.
>
> After getting up, I leave the apartment and get my bike from the basement. As I go outside I notice a large luxury car, which I associate with speed, selfishness, environmental damage and a large ego. I notice that the car is blocking a fire hydrant ... stop ... where am I? My thoughts are preoccupied with anger, self-justification and self-righeousness. I decide to choose not to let my thoughts run away with me on this journey, but rather to use the rest of the commute to look, listen and experience the journey. The first thing I notice is the coolness of the early morning. As I continue riding my bike I notice the gentle bumps as I cycle over cobblestones. I look at the bright lights in the windows and hear the rustle of leaves on the ground as I go

past. I see and feel my hands around the handlebars and notice the movement of my thighs and how my feet feel on the pedals. I pass a river which is lined with many trees and I think I can hear a bird chirping. Hearing the birds chirping triggers an inner smile. After a while, I notice that I'm back in my mind and have been thinking about memories of a recent workshop which was challenging. I find myself in an imaginary dialogue with the participants, in which I justify my behaviour. As I notice this, I let go of those memories and bring my attention back to my body. I notice the cooling wind, the feeling of holding the handlebars, and my legs moving. I notice the sounds of the cars around me and a gentle chugging sound coming from a large truck, which sounds so different from the gentle hum of the cars. I notice the clicking of boots as I pass someone walking on the footpath and the hum of a small car as it weaves its way through the morning traffic. I remember that I need to create a list of lecturers and send out the list as agreed.

I come to a red light and have to wait. I direct my attention to my breathing and the sensations in the soles of my feet as they rest on the road, while I'm standing. I feel my breathing is faster and deeper as a result of the exercise. I notice this feeling seems to make its way down to my stomach. The traffic light turns green. I cycle along the road and reach a bridge. As I cycle over I pass a number of joggers and notice the gentle pitter patter of their steps and become aware that several joggers seem to be breathing heavily. Ducks sleep with their heads under their wings on the surface of the river. As I cycle around a curve, I notice leaves falling from the trees in a clockwise, spiral motion. Shortly after, I find myself thinking about another therapist, angry at how she behaved. I find myself in a mental dispute with her … stop. I move my attention back again to my hands and notice my face, the cobblestone street, the vibration of the tyres and the buzz of the cars around me in the here and now. Suddenly, I'm gripped by a horrible feeling. I lose control of my bike for a moment. I regain control and continue on. The traffic light turns yellow and I feel the impulse

121

to speed up to get through it before it turns red. The memory of being fined by the police because they thought I'd gone through a red light comes to mind. That was a big fine. This triggers the thought that in Germany you can lose your driver's licence for bad behaviour on your bike. I am a good driver, but when I'm on my bike I'm more likely to take risks due to the minimal danger to third parties. Stop … again … I'm caught in a self-justifying narrative mode. I'm only a few hundred metres from my work place. I feel the chill of the autumn air, my hands on the handlebars, the rhythmic moving of my legs and notice how the sky is slowly becoming brighter as it becomes daylight. As I arrive at work, I get off my bike and hear my keys clink together as I pull them out of my pocket. I notice how my hands feel as I rotate the key in the lock. I hear the garage door roll open. Mentally, I note 'done'. I feel proud of myself for managing to stay focused on my journey. I have tried this before, but this is the first time I've made it the whole way without becoming lost in thought. Reflecting on the process, I realise that the conscious direction to listen and notice my body, and naming my 'self-talk', helped me come back to the present again and again.

Try it out for yourself!

COFFEE MACHINE TAI CHI

The daily preparation of coffee or tea in the office can also become a mindfulness exercise. Here is an example from one of the authors.

In our institute we have a coffee machine. I often fill it in the morning because I'm usually the first one to arrive. I have a regular routine; I open up the metal coffee pot, dispose of the old coffee, rinse the pot, make sure I wash away any remains of coffee in the sink. I then shut the pot, open the filter, and throw the used filter in the rubbish. I then open the cabinet and get out a new filter from the box and take out the coffee can. I measure out the coffee and place it in the machine. I measure out the right amount of water in a measuring cup and then put it in the machine, close the lid and press start. The coffee machine is slightly defective and doesn't always start straight away. I notice my own irritation as I reflect on the fact that the warranty has only just expired, then keep pressing the button until it starts. Sometimes the coffee machine starts, sometimes it shuts itself down. Now that I use this as a mindfulness practice I no longer get irritated by the process and in fact, I hope we don't get a new coffee machine too soon!

You might be wondering where the Tai Chi comes in! As I go through the routine outlined above, I always make sure I use my whole body and that my shoulders, elbows and wrists do not twist. Because this activity happens in a small space it is possible to make all the actions flow together as one graceful movement. I also try to bring all the objects to the mid-line of my body. Even pouring the coffee can be a coffee Tai Chi exercise, as you pay attention to the coffee pot and the coffee cup and centre the body and the movement.

THE TEA MASTER

While I was still a student I had the opportunity to participate in an authentic Japanese tea ceremony at a museum. The tea master accidentally spilt the water on his kimono, which left a large water mark. He soon settled from the disruption and continued on with the ceremony harmoniously. At the time, I remember thinking, somewhat sarcastically, 'Well how careless'. Today, I reassess the tea master story. Mindfulness is simply not a high-performance sport in which we are judged as to how mindful we are and endeavour to get a 'perfect ten'. Rather it is about being in the present, with an attitude of acceptance for what unfolds. The tea master spills the water, notes the spilling, perhaps noticing internal thoughts such as 'What will people think?', before letting go of those thoughts and turning his attention to completing the tea ceremony. In mindfulness, and in life, it is fruitless to expend energy aiming for perfection. It is far more productive to accept that perfection is impossible and to focus on 'getting up again' when you fall.

4.2.2 Uncertainty experiment

This exercise deals with uncertainty (based on Wilson, 2008, pp. 133–135). Allow about an hour for this. Prepare something to eat – perhaps a salad, slice of bread, or even something hot. If you choose something hot, keep in mind that you either need to be prepared to eat it cold, or have facilities to heat it up once it becomes cold. Put your food on the table and ensure that you will really commit to one hour for this practice. Start with the idea that you do not really know whether you want to eat the food or not. Stay with this uncertainty and observe your internal decision-making processes – 'No, not now' or 'Yes, I want to eat now'. Sit down and just observe. Every so often you might like to review your latest decision. Stay in this state of uncertainty and notice your physical reactions. Notice the back-and-forth process and evaluate the situation. Perhaps you think to yourself 'What nonsense' and judge the exercise. Remember the goal of the experiment is not to decide one way or another in the first half an hour. At the end of the experiment you will choose either to eat the food, or to wrap it up and eat it later. The purpose of the experiment is to show how much we depend on clear decisions in everyday life and what it feels like not to know and have more options available.

This 'Do-not-know mind' can be helpful in your work with others. Perhaps in our certainty about the right way forward you have closed your mind to other possibilities.

4.2.3 *Reflection on your life*

While we practise mindfulness with the hope of staying grounded in the present, sometimes our internal narratives can be helpful. These can be individual, familial, national or cultural narratives. For the following exercises, explore your individual and familial narratives and how they impact you.

FROM THE BEGINNING

Begin this exercise by grounding yourself in the here and now. Say your name to yourself. Feel your body. Try to imagine what you look like from the outside. Bring your attention back to your body and feel your breath as you say to yourself, 'This is me now.' Imagine yourself as a baby. This image might be informed by photos, stories your parents or grandparents told, or your idea of what it means to be a baby. Say to yourself 'This is little...'. Use your first and last names. Take a moment to enjoy this mental picture. Then jump to the here and now. How did you get from being a baby to today? Notice what key milestones and events come to mind. What was helpful? What hindered you? What are you particularly proud of? There is no fixed schedule for this, but you might like to include your early childhood, kindergarten, primary school, secondary school, university or vocational training, professional activities, or personal milestones, such as friendships, relationships, separations, deaths, marriages or births. The whole thing may be a mosaic, it is up to you. If you run out of ideas, imagine yourself as a baby or toddler and say 'This is little...', then visualise yourself at an older age and say 'This is young...'. And just observe what emerges spontaneously. After you feel you have done this for long enough, release all the images and notice what impact this exercise has had on you. If you like, you can spend some time just noticing what emerges and naming any sensations, thoughts or feelings in simple words. To end this exercise, sit for at least five minutes and focus on your breathing. You can follow your breath or you might like to count each exhalation from one to ten and then repeat.

The aim of the exercise is to help us to realise how strongly the past determines our experience and feelings in the present, and how past experiences can be reactivated quickly, simply by thinking about them. We all know from our own experience that environmental cues can trigger earlier episodes and influence our thinking and feeling.

To illustrate just this point, the Buddhist meditation teacher Thích Nhất Hạnh has designed a beautiful picture presenting all these experiences as seeds, in a so-called store-consciousness, which germinate when they are watered.

VIEWS: FROM THE END

There is only one absolute certainty in life, that we must all die. During the Middle Ages, a memento mori, a constant awareness of death, was quite common. Our contemporary society is quite different in that we suppress thoughts of our own death. Death is generally only mentioned in the media when it is the result of violence or a natural disaster. The following exercise is a revision of one presented by Covey (2004). It provides us with an opportunity, here and now, to reflect on our values and what is important to us.

Imagine that you have lived to a ripe old age and died peacefully. What would your friends and acquaintances say about you? What would your loved ones say about you? What would you hope that people would remember about you? You might like to consider how people from different areas of your life may respond. Imagine what each of the following people would say:

1. Your spouse, or if you have no spouse, your closest friend.
2. Your children, or if you don't have children, maybe people you have supported over a long period of time.

3. Family members, e.g., mother, father, brother, auntie, and so forth. If your parents are already deceased, you can imagine the spirits of your parents at your grave.

If you like, you can specify the exercise so that each person says:

'I would like to thank _____.'
'He has enriched my life by _____.'
'He has helped me by _____.'

You can also reframe this so as to ask yourself: How do I want to live from now on, so that people can say that about me? Don't write this down, just think it through. Mentally visualise the sentences. Finish the exercise with the questions 'How is my body, how is my mood?' and 'Does this practice have implications for the way I want to live my life?'

To close, raise your palms in front of your face. The left hand is the representative of the past. Move it to the left. The right hand, which stands for the future, move to the right. Then rub the palms of both hands together. Feel the heat that is created, in the here and now, by bringing the two together.

References

Covey, S. R. (2004). *The 7 habits of highly effective people*. New York: Free Press.

Wilson, K. G. (2008). *Mindfulness for two: An acceptance and commitment therapy approach to mindfulness in psychotherapy*. Oakland, CA: New Harbinger Publications.

4.3 Mindfulness Exercises for the Helping Role

In this section we focus on mindfulness exercises which can be used in the workplace. In addition to helping you personally, as mentioned in Chapter 2, there is evidence that mindfulness may help you to improve the quality of your work (Grepmair and Nickel, 2007) and developing your own practice is an essential prerequisite for using mindfulness-based therapies with your clients (Rimes and Wingrove, 2011).

Beginning your day

Your chair can be used as an important trigger to remember to be mindful. When you arrive in the morning, sit for a moment with your eyes closed and run through your day so far. You got up, perhaps had a drink or breakfast, got to work and now find yourself sitting in your chair. You might like to consider any thoughts or feelings you have about the day ahead. Then take a moment to consider your posture and breathing. Take ten breaths, consciously, counting each exhalation. When you have finished this, consider how you will feel at the end of the working day. How will your body feel?

Greeting your patient

At the beginning of the day you might like to lay out the records of the clients you will be seeing, in order. Before the client comes in take a moment to check in with yourself and what has happened in the last hour. Then quickly take a minute to scan the client's record and perhaps even visualise the client. As you hold this image in your mind, with a sense of empathy, agree to greet your patient with fresh eyes and be prepared to update your ideas and assessments of your client.

Then let go of all the images and greet your client. As you greet your client, feel your feet on the ground as you make eye contact with them.

Attention to your voice

The way one speaks is important. You can, for example, use a particular tone or softness, which may influence the meaning of what is said. The same applies to pauses in speech. It is useful to be clear that speech is more than just the sounds of language; it is also the pauses and silences. For example, speaking continuously without a break would result in your words starting to run into one another and sounding a bit whiney. The breaks between words are powerful. See if you can pay attention to the empty space around the words when talking to your clients. The same can be done with your clients' speech. Where do your clients rest, where are they silent?

Dealing with silence

It is interesting to note how clients respond if you are silent. Some clients find this very aversive. It's worth discussing this with your clients to see if they are agreeable to you using small silences as breaks, to digest what has just been said. If you have a client who experiences social anxiety, make sure you discuss this with that client, in detail, as the client may quickly feel social pressure to 'fill the gap'.

The therapist and therapy-induced emotions

Mindful awareness allows you to be aware of thoughts and emotions that arise during the session, such as anger, shame, erotic interest and sexual impulses, boredom, disgust and disapproval. During the session it is useful to notice what emerges, before releasing it and returning your focus to your client. However, after the session, it may be useful to reflect on what emerged. Were the thoughts or feelings based on your own feelings? Are they your issues that were triggered by your client? Or, are they feelings or thoughts that emerged from the interaction with your client and represent your client's issues?

Regenerating mindfulness exercises for the therapist in an hour

Working with others can be considered a sort of 'emotional labour', and it is up to you to ensure that you make time to relax and recharge your batteries – especially if you're working intensively with clients. Here are two exercises that may help.

Take a moment to become aware of your body as you sit in your chair. Notice your feet on the ground, bottom on the chair, and ensure you're sitting upright and your body is relaxed. We often just 'put up' with being uncomfortable! Release any tension in your neck, shoulders, or anywhere else you notice tension. It is important to take the time to be as comfortable as possible.

Another exercise may be particularly helpful if your client unexpectedly or violently launches a verbal attack on you. It is natural to find that jarring, irritating or upsetting. The following three steps might be helpful:

1. Notice what emerges.
2. Rename it with a simple word (such as anger, fear).
3. Use your breath. For very intense emotions taking deep breaths and holding your breath and counting to ten is also useful. After holding your breath, gently transition

atmosphere was created. In the first part of the hour I had felt disappointed that she was experiencing problems again, and annoyance at the working conditions she faced, alongside a sense of urgency to come up with a solution for her. As the hour progressed, this changed, as space for reflection allowed her to determine the appropriate actions for herself.

Turn down the sound

We tend to give what our clients say much more weight than their non-verbal communication. If you're watching video recordings of sessions it can be useful to turn down the sound and notice what your clients are saying with their body language. During a session you might like to try paying more attention to the non-verbal cues from your clients. What gestures do they make? What sort of facial expressions? Try looking at your clients with fresh eyes and notice what you see.

At the end

At the end of a session you might realise that you've tensed up, or feel emotional or distracted. You might like to use a moment of mindfulness to close your sessions. Try your own version of the following:

'Now our time has come to an end, I invite you to notice how you feel. Be aware of any thoughts, feelings, or emotions.'

Take a moment to discuss what your client says. Then end the session by asking your client what they feel they are able to take away from the session.

Exercise at the end of the workday

At the end of the day, sit back in your chair and ask yourself 'Do I feel tension in my body? If so, where? What emotions am I aware of? What thoughts or images present themselves? Do I carry any thoughts of my clients or colleagues with me?' Then, feel a wave of relaxation go through your body from the top of your head, to your face, shoulders, chest, abdomen, bottom, thighs, lower legs and feet. As the wave reaches your feet, imagine any negativity or stress draining away from them. Then let the relaxation wave flow back up to your head again. Repeat this cycle as many times as you like. You might find it useful to set a timer for five minutes or so for this exercise. When you finish, take a moment to consider how you feel.

It can be difficult for therapists, who spend their working days listening and supporting others, to leave work and go home to the expectations of partners, family and friends. This exercise can help the therapist to refresh himself at the end of the working day.

Another exercise that might be useful is to stand with your arms open wide and visualise greeting your partner or children when you return home. Some therapists who have tried this have reported imagining their children or partner greeting them with a warm embrace. Of course, the reality when you return home may be quite different. Again, this is an opportunity to practise mindfulness.

Something a little different

The integration of mindfulness meditation and visualisation is common in Tibetan Buddhism. Many meditation exercises involve imagining images of particular deities and involve the meditator beginning to identify with the qualities of the deities (Wallace, 1993). This centuries-old practice aims at supporting meditators to develop positive qualities such as love, wisdom and compassion. The mindfulness teacher Thích Nhất Hạnh also uses visualisations with images or verbal prompts (Hạnh, 1998). Given this background, we feel justified in including the following, despite the fact it isn't a formal mindfulness exercise but rather aims at bringing latent memories or attitudes to mind.

Every therapist has memories of moments in their work where things went particularly well, not just in terms of the progress of the client, but also in terms of their own development. It is all too easy to focus on what is not going well, or on past mistakes. The purpose of the following exercise is to do the exact opposite – to focus on things that *have* gone well.

Call to mind a time when you felt as though you were at your most competent, or when you made an important advance with a client, or perhaps a time when you were praised in front of your colleagues. Try to reconnect with this memory – try to connect with the situation as much as you can. Let the pleasant feelings of gratitude and pride wash over you and 'bathe' in the mental and physical sensations for a moment. Then let go of the scene. You might like to say 'Let go' to yourself internally. Then turn your attention to your breathing for a few moments and notice if the pleasant feeling or positive memories linger on. Let them be there, but do not focus on them.

Visualisation of specific qualities, power sources or models

In preparation for this exercise, please compile a list of some of the qualities you feel are particularly helpful for you in your work. A typical list might include things like patience, calmness, stability, boldness, confidence and empathy. Select a quality from this list or one of your own. Now think of someone who you feel embodies this quality. This could be a colleague, a trainer or even someone from the literature. Once you have decided upon the person, bring that person to mind and state that quality internally to yourself. Sit with this for a few moments. Feel that quality within you, supporting you. If it seems useful to you, you might like to imagine the person supporting you, perhaps putting a hand on your shoulder. Let this image stabilise for a few moments, then say goodbye to the person. If you like, you can express gratitude. Return your attention to your breath and do your favourite breathing exercise. Let the image linger if you wish, but remember not to focus on it.

Reflecting on failures

Over the course of your working life there are likely to be a few clients you will remember with regret, and believe, perhaps rightly, that you would do things differently now. It can be useful to reflect on negative results in therapy. Sometimes it is useful to examine your own weaknesses to enable you to work on overcoming them.

Visualise a client–therapist interaction that was difficult, and you felt could not be saved. Sit with this image or feeling and observe, without judging or evaluating. When you become aware of mental chatter, notice these thoughts and feelings, let them go and observe the image. To finish, praise yourself for your courage to examine areas where you feel you have not performed well. By recognising, and 'forgiving' yourself for your fallibility and imperfection, you pave the way for improvement.

In-depth representation of current clients

From time to time you might find it useful to use the following exercise as a form of 'self-supervison':

1. Bring an image of your client to mind and let it stabilise for a moment.
2. Notice any triggers which may appear. What physical sensations, emotions, thoughts or impulses do you notice?
3. Consider the image of your client. What comes to mind? Notice whatever presents itself. Let the image of your client be there and stabilise for a few moments. Let go of the picture and ask yourself what personal qualities you need to work successfully with this client.

Those who have attended our courses report that this exercise can be shortened so it can also be used before each session.

Acceptance of weaknesses and 'bad habits'

The aim of this exercise is to realise that becoming mindful of our weaknesses may help us transform them into strengths. We use the idea that we can interpret weakness as 'strengths and skills in the wrong place'. In other words: Strength in the wrong place is a weakness. This weakness (used in the right way, at the right time and in the right place) can be transformed into a strength. In this playful approach, you might like to list one to three weaknesses.

The following is an example given by a participant at one of our courses. He reported the following weaknesses: he was impatient, felt bored sometimes and got annoyed when clients didn't adhere to their support plans. However, he also felt a lot of solidarity with his clients if they were treated badly. Participants at one of our groups developed the following list for themselves:

1. Impatience and awareness may lead him to reflect deeply on what is possible and help him to really appreciate small positive changes in his client, which would then serve to reinforce that change is possible.
2. Feeling bored was another key issue. He could sit with the boredom and let it be there while he focused on his physical presence, his breathing, which in turn would bring him into the present moment and lead him back to his client.
3. In relation to the anger, the group suggested that the anger over the mistreatment of his client by a third party could be addressed by consciously observing and feeling concrete actions that might be helpful for the patient. It would more difficult to deal with anger relating to clients who arrived late or didn't complete their home practice. The group suggested that it was helpful to reflect on the client's goals as a first step.

Mindful speech

The challenge of mindful speech for us, as therapists, is to take a closer look at how we talk about our clients between our-selves and with third parties. Mindful speech also challenges us to examine how we speak to ourselves. Of course, examining our language isn't unique to mindfulness approaches. Many of the things mentioned here are likely to be in keeping with the 'irrational thoughts' outlined by Albert Ellis (1977) or the 'thinking errors' described by Beck et al. (1993). It might be useful to use the following questions as a guide to get you started exam-ining your use of language (see Wilson, 2008, pp. 125–148):

- Am I using morally loaded language?
- Am I using 'should' in my speech or my self-talk?
- Am I considering the clients as individuals or thinking of them by the label of their diagnoses?
- Am I blaming the client?
- Am I describing the client's behaviour as manipulative, divisive or damaging to therapy?

Maybe you'd like to keep a note of some of your verbal patterns over the coming few weeks? Reflecting on these points can help you to increase your flexibility and be aware of the expectations and judgments you bring to your work. This keeps the door open for things to be different.

References

Beck, A. T., Rush, A. J., Shaw, B. E., & Emery, G. (1993). *Kognitive Therapie der Depression (3. Aufl.)*. Weinheim: Beltz.

Ellis, A. (1977). *Die Rational-emotive Therapie: Das innere Selbstgespräch bei seelischen Problemen und seine Veränderung*. Munich: Pfeiffer.

Grepmair, L. J., & Nickel, M. K. (2007). *Achtsamkeit des Psychotherapeuten*. Vienna: Springer.

Hạnh, T. N. (1998). *Und ich blühe wie eine Blume. Geführte Meditationen und Lieder (2. Aufl.)*. Braunschweig: Aurum.

Rimes, K. A., & Wingrove, J. (2011). Pilot study of mindfulness-based cognitive therapy for trainee clinical psychologists. *Behavioural and Cognitive Psychotherapy, 39*, 235.

Wallace, A. B. (1993). *Tibetan Buddhism from the ground up: A practical approach for modern life*. Sommerville: Wisdom Publications.

Wilson, K. G. (2008). *Mindfulness for two: An acceptance and commitment therapy approach to mindfulness in psychotherapy*. Oakland, CA: New Harbinger Publications.

4.4 Mindful Moments With Your Clients

Even if you originally started reading this book purely for personal reasons, after having established (or extended) your own practice you may be curious about using mindfulness with your clients.

If you are interested in using mindfulness with your clients formally, either in groups or one to one, we strongly suggest you seek out a formal mindfulness teacher training programme. There are lots of established training routes for programmes such as Mindfulness-Based Stress Reduction, Mindfulness-Based Cognitive Therapy, and the Breathworks Mindfulness for Health programme.

The purpose of this short section is to outline how you can use mindfulness exercises in your sessions to support the other therapeutic approaches you are using.

Starting the session

We feel that the first step to incorporating mindfulness into your therapeutic work is to establish your own practice and bring that mindful presence to your interactions with your clients. By doing this, you are also modelling a mindful approach for your clients. You could choose to incorporate mindful pauses into your sessions, as you feel they are appropriate. This isn't to 'teach mindfulness', but rather to create a mindful environment for the session. For example, you could try some variation of the following:

> Let's just pause for a moment and notice the weight of the feet on the floor and the weight of the body as we sit. Notice any muscle tension or discomfort and remember it's fine to move a

little. How is the breath? There is no need to change anything, just notice what is there. Are you aware of any sounds? What else do you notice? Now, just come back to the room and open your eyes, if you closed them. How was that?

This exercise should take around three minutes.

In our experience, it is useful to explain the concept of mindfulness to clients as it helps them understand the benefits and, importantly, that it is normal to be distracted by thoughts, feelings, noises, and so forth.

Introducing mindfulness

You might find it helpful to utilise images, quotations or even poems to help your client understand the concept of mindfulness. For example, the following poem is frequently used in mindfulness circles as a way of explaining what it means to be mindful. How do you interpret it?

The Guest House

This being human is a guest house.
Every morning a new arrival.

A joy, a depression, a meanness,
some momentary awareness comes
as an unexpected visitor.

Welcome and entertain them all!
Even if they are a crowd of sorrows,
who violently sweep your house
empty of its furniture,
still, treat each guest honourably.
He may be clearing you out
for some new delight.

The dark thought, the shame, the malice.
meet them at the door laughing and invite them in.

Be grateful for whatever comes.
because each has been sent
as a guide from beyond.

Rumi

Awareness of the five senses

In keeping with its title, this exercise is about bringing your client's attention to the five senses. It is particularly helpful if you want to help your client to shift focus from the inner experience to the outer world.

Invite your client to bring each of the five senses to the forefront of their attention, one at a time, and provide a few prompts as you see fit. We usually begin with seeing, followed by hearing, touching, smelling and tasting. There are plenty of visual stimuli in any office (plants, carpets, books, pens, chairs), although it can be slightly more difficult to direct attention to sounds. However, if you pay close attention you will probably observe sounds such as the rustling of paper, the creaking of floorboards or the crackling of a heater. For the sense of touch, you could focus on the pressure of the feet on the ground, the weight of a wristwatch or perhaps the touch of a shirt collar. The senses of smell and taste can be difficult, but be free to open up the possibility that the client may not smell or taste anything in particular. The entire exercise can take five to ten minutes.

This exercise seems to reduce tension in most clients we have used it with and is a way of grounding the client in their physical environment.

Closing the session

A mindfulness exercise can also be a useful way of bringing sessions to an end. For example, you could try some variation of the following:

> Now, we've come to the end of the session, how do you feel right now? Notice how it feels to be sitting on your chair. Is there any stress or tension in your body? Are you aware of any particular thoughts?

After a bit of a pause, you could ask:

> What have you discovered? What are you taking away from today?

Then bring the session to a close.

5

Short Manual for Running a Group Based on the Presented Material

This manual is designed for:

- Those of you who already have some sort of mindfulness teacher training certificate, or extensive meditation experience.
- Those of you who would like to use the material as a form of peer support and reflection. You could do the same thing with any meditation book and CD, except this material is tailored to your needs.

The manual should be used in conjunction with the material in Chapter 3. It is presumed that before you lead anyone else through this material that you will have worked through it yourself, and be familiar with the meditations and activities.

Mindfulness for Therapists: Understanding Mindfulness for Professional Effectiveness and Personal Well-Being, First Edition. Gerhard Zarbock, Siobhan Lynch, Axel Ammann and Silka Ringer.
Companion Website: www.wiley.com/go/zarbock/mindfulnessfortherapists

You can use the recorded meditations that are available online (www.wiley.com/go/zarbock/mindfulnessfortherapists).

General Notes on Implementation

The course consists of eight weekly sessions and a mindfulness day. The duration of the weekly meetings should be at least 90 minutes. Depending on how many people are in your group it might be useful to have longer sessions of 150 minutes. This ensures plenty of time for discussion, questions and breaks. If you run out of time for an exercise, in a given week, you can either add the exercise to a future session or practise it during the mindfulness day.

Please note that the home practice we have outlined is intended as a suggestion only. There is a fine balance between promoting the regular home practice and overloading participants. It is better to practise a few exercises regularly than a lot occasionally. Regular practice will result in feelings of success, even if that success is small. Such a feeling of success is an essential motivator to continue with the regular practice.

Leading the group

It is helpful if the person facilitating the group is able to take a few minutes before the group begins to 'tune in'. This isn't easy! We suggest the facilitator incorporates time to practise a short mindfulness exercise before the group. This exercise, which is similar to Exercise 5 (Flash mindfulness), may be useful:

Make sure you will be undisturbed for a few minutes before the group session begins. You can do this standing, sitting or lying down. We suggest you close your eyes if this is comfortable for you. What thoughts are dominant at the moment?

Examine them for a moment without judging them. What emotions are you aware of? How is your body? What do you notice? Something pleasant? Something unpleasant? On a scale of 0–100, with 0 being not tense at all and 100 being extremely tense, how tense are you? Bring your attention to your breath for a minute or so. When you're ready, expand your awareness and become aware of your body as a whole. Do this for another minute or so. If you're feeling particularly tense, it might be a good idea to do this for a little longer. Become aware of the immediate future and the mindfulness session. From the second session onwards you might like to tune in and recall how you felt at the end of the last session. Take a deep breath and open your eyes.

At the end of the session

Reflect on what has just taken place. Did the session have a particular 'flavour'? This could emerge in the form of feelings or physical sensations. You might be aware of particular thoughts or even sentences about the session. Notice what emerges and name them. You might notice areas where things didn't go as you had planned, or where things went particularly well. After reflecting on these points for a few moments, let go of them and turn your attention to your breath for a minute. Then carry on with the rest of your day.

Week 1: Introduction to Mindfulness

Structure of Week 1

1. Pre-exercise 'What is there?' (10 mins)
2. Welcome and introduction (5)

3. Group introductions (10)
4. Structure of the programme (5)
5. Experiential focus (5)
6. Introducing mindfulness (15)
7. Breath concentration (5)
8. The concept of concentration (10)
9. Seated mindfulness (10)
10. Mindfulness in everyday life: Home practice (10)
11. Questions (5)

Materials

- Singing bowl (or a bell)
- Timer
- Name tags
- Small cards, pens, pins/adhesive to put cards up

1. Exercise 1: 'What is there?'

Begin by explaining to the group that this is the introductory exercise and ask them to get comfortable. It may be useful to invite them to close their eyes if they wish. Guide the group through Exercise 1 (Chapter 3.1). Before you begin, explain that the exercise will end when you ring the bell. The exercise should last approximately ten minutes. After the exercise ask the participants to jot down a few notes regarding their experiences of the exercise. Explain to them that there will be some time to share their experiences with the group during the introductions.

2. Welcome and introduction (facilitators)

The formal session begins with the facilitators of the group introducing themselves briefly.

- Name
- Area of expertise
- Own experience of mindfulness
- Own motivation for facilitating the group

3. Group introductions

Ask each participant to give their name, some brief feedback on their experience of the introductory exercise and their motivation for attending the programme.

4. Structure of the programme

Themes of each week:

- Week 1: Introduction to mindfulness
- Week 2: The five elements of mindfulness
- Week 3: Integrating mindfulness into everyday life
- Week 4: Mindfulness as a way of life
- Week 5: Mindfulness as a home base for therapists
- Week 6: Mindfulness of the body
- Week 7: Integrating mindfulness into therapeutic practice
- Week 8: Review and next steps
- Your oasis

5. Experiential focus

Explain to the group that this programme takes an experiential approach to helping participants discover or deepen their understanding of mindfulness. We have chosen to keep the theoretical explanations to an absolute minimum in the hope of helping them discover the benefits for themselves.

6. Introducing mindfulness

Mindfulness is becoming a familiar term to therapists, yet this term may mean different things to different people. As a starting point for discussing mindfulness, a group exercise may be useful. Ask the participants to write down on some small cards a brief example of a time they feel they have been mindful. Put all the cards up on the wall or a notice board so everyone can see them. Discuss some of the similarities and differences and use this as the foundation for Kabat-Zinn's common definition of mindfulness, and introduce:

- Monkey mind
- Five elements of mindfulness
- Self-resonance
- First-, second- and third-person perspective

Links are made throughout the programme between the theoretical concepts and personal experience, so there is no need to spend too long on this in the first session.

7. Breath concentration

Guide participants through Exercise 2 (Chapter 3.1).

8. The concept of concentration

Ask the participants how they found Exercise 2. Based on the participant feedback, make the point that it is often very difficult to concentrate for any length of time and discuss the central role concentration plays in mindfulness meditation (Chapter 2). It is particularly important to emphasise that it is perfectly normal if their minds wander off after a few breaths. Following on from this discussion, guide participants through Exercise 4 (Chapter 3.1). Afterwards, ask them how they found it.

9. Seated mindfulness

Guide participants through Exercise 3 (Finding your relaxed, upright position, Chapter 3.1) to help them find a relaxed position for meditation. Follow this with Exercise 4 (Seated mindfulness, Chapter 3.1).

10. Mindfulness in everyday life: Home practice

Make it clear to participants that the exercises can be divided into two groups: exercises which they are asked to practise regularly throughout the programme, and those they practise in a certain week to illustrate a particular aspect of mindfulness.

It is worth allowing plenty of time to discuss the importance of regular home practice and setting up a regular spot to practise. Allow enough time to help participants find their own 'relaxed, upright position'. This seems very simple, but finding the right position can make a big difference to how participants feel about settling down to practise.

Introduce Exercise 5 (Flash mindfulness, Chapter 3.1) and the daily meditation diaries.

Exercises for the week ahead:

- Exercise 5: Flash mindfulness (three times daily).
- Mindfulness diary (daily).
- Exercise 2: Breath concentration (daily, minimum of five minutes).
- Exercise 4: Seated mindfulness (daily, minimum of five minutes).

11. Questions

Leave plenty of time for questions and discussion at the end of the session.

Week 2: The Five Elements of Mindfulness

Structure of Week 2

1. Welcome (5 mins)
2. Flash mindfulness (5)
3. The week in review (15)
4. Pre-tree (10)
5. Singing bowl meditation (15)
6. Listening: Observing and naming (10)
7. Non-judgmental description (15)
8. Home practice (5)
9. Questions (5)
10. Flash mindfulness (5)

Materials

- Singing bowl
- Timer
- Name tags

1. Welcome

Welcome the group and ensure everyone has everything they need for the session.

2. Flash mindfulness

After you have guided the participants through Exercise 5 (Chapter 3.1), explain that each session will begin and end with this exercise.

3. The week in review

Ask the participants how they got on with their homework over the last week. Ask what went well, what difficulties they experienced and how they reacted. You could do this as a group or in pairs.

4. Pre-tree

Go through Exercise 6 (Chapter 3.2) with participants and allow time for feedback at the end.

5. Singing bowl meditation

The purpose of this exercise is to help your participants become more aware of sounds. Strike the singing bowl and listen to the sound until it has faded away completely. Then, strike it again. Continue doing this. You could try leaving a slightly longer silence before each strike of the bowl. For an outline of the exercise, see below. We did not include it in Chapter 3 as it is more suited to a group environment.

Sitting down, ensure that you are in a relaxed upright position, with your hands resting on your lap or your knees. You may close your eyes or keep them slightly open and look down towards the ground in front of you. Let the sound of the singing bowl become the focus of your attention. Perhaps you are aware of the changing sound of the singing bowl as the sound gradually fades and then disappears. If you get distracted by other thoughts or feelings, just let them be there and focus your attention on the sound of the singing bowl. The sound waves are a little like ripples on a lake after a stone has been thrown in. The waves are large at first but get smaller and smaller until they are barely perceptible. Eventually they disappear altogether and the surface of the lake is perfectly calm. Bringing this exercise to a close, become aware of your body and then open your eyes when you're ready.

6. Listening: Observing and naming

Guide the participants through Exercise 7 (Chapter 3.2). After the exercise ask participants what they noticed. Use their feedback as the basis for discussing the importance of observing and naming sounds, thoughts and feelings without judging them.

7. Non-judgmental description

Ask participants to get into pairs and guide them through Exercise 8 (Chapter 3.2). After the exercise ask the participants to stay in their pairs and discuss how they found the exercise.

8. Home practice

Remind the participants about the importance of regular home practice. It might be useful to discuss any difficulties as a group and come up with possible solutions together.

- Exercise 5: Flash mindfulness. For the rest of the programme expand the Flash mindfulness exercise by asking: What was the most attentive moment of the day? What was the most careless moment of the day? What physical sensations were evoked in each of these moments? (three times daily).
- Mindfulness diary (daily).
- Exercise 7: Auditory field (three times in the week, minimum of five minutes). You might like to practise Exercise 7, or the Flash mindfulness, in the relaxed sitting

position (see Week 1, Exercise 3). This will help you to prepare for the sitting exercises next week.

* Exercise 8: Non-judgmental description (three times in the week, minimum of 15 minutes).

9. Questions

Ask participants if they have any final questions or issues they would like to discuss.

10. Flash mindfulness

Use Exercise 5 (Chapter 3.1) to close the session.

Week 3: Integrating Mindfulness into Everyday Life

Structure of Week 3

1. Welcome (5 mins)
2. Flash mindfulness (5)
3. The week in review (15)
4. Energise (20)
5. Sitting meditation (20)
6. Integration into everyday life (15)
7. Questions (5)
8. Flash mindfulness (5)

Materials

* Singing bowl
* Timer

1. Welcome

2. Flash mindfulness (Exercise 5, Chapter 3.1)

3. The week in review

4. Energise

Introduce the participants to Exercise 10 (Chapter 3.3). Explain to participants that this exercise can help them become more in tune with their bodies, while also re-energising them if they feel particularly drained.

5. Sitting meditation

Introduce participants to the sitting meditation by guiding them through Exercise 11 (Chapter 3.3). After the exercise ask participants to share their experiences with the group. Use this feedback as the basis for discussing the importance of non-reacting (Chapter 2, Chapter 3.3).

6. Integration into everyday life

Any activity can be a meditation if approached in a mindful way. Ask the participants to consider how they could integrate mindfulness into their lives. In which situations would it be helpful? What challenges are there? You could do this as a larger group or split participants up into small groups or pairs.

Once they have come up with their own ideas, you might like to guide the group through Exercise 7 (Chapter 3.2).

7. Home practice

- Exercise 5: Flash mindfulness (three times daily).
- Mindfulness diary (daily).
- Exercise 11: Sitting meditation (three times in the week).
- Make time to observe daily activities/situations in a focused and non-judgmental way.

8. Questions

Allow time for any questions on the material.

9. Flash mindfulness

Use Exercise 5 (Chapter 3.1) to close the session.

Week 4: Mindfulness as a Way of Life

Structure of Week 4

1. Welcome (5 mins)
2. Flash mindfulness (5)
3. The week in review (15)
4. Automatic pilot (30)
5. Leaves on a river (15)
6. In a nutshell (5)
7. Home practice (5)
8. Questions (5)
9. Flash mindfulness (5)

Materials

- Singing bowl
- Timer

1. Welcome

2. Flash mindfulness (Exercise 5, Chapter 3.1)

3. The week in review

4. Non-reacting

Begin with a short exercise. Ask the participants to get together in pairs. For two minutes, one person describes the other (e.g. You have blue eyes, a small nose, grey hair, etc.). The other person just listens for two minutes, in silence. The listener's task is to listen and notice any reactions to what the other person says. The roles are then reversed. After this exercise give each pair a few minutes to talk to one another about the experience, then ask the pairs to feed back to the group. The feedback from this exercise can be used as the basis for a deeper discussion of the concept of non-reacting in everyday life (Chapter 2, Chapter 3.4).

After this exercise, lead the participants through Exercise 13 (Sitting meditation with 'non-responsiveness', Chapter 3.4).

5. Leaves on a river

Lead participants through Exercise 14 (Chapter 3.4). Afterwards invite participants to share how they found it. Building on the comments, discuss how this exercise could be used in participants' working lives.

6. In a nutshell

Introduce Exercise 15 (Chapter 3.4). Open a discussion about when it might be useful to use this exercise.

158

7. Home practice

- Exercise 5: Flash mindfulness (three times daily).
- Mindfulness diary (daily).
- Exercise 13: Sitting meditation (daily, minimum 15 minutes).
- Experiment with the non-reacting exercises (at least three times in the week).
- Reflect on your own needs (daily).

8. Questions

9. Flash mindfulness to close

Week 5: Mindfulness as a Home Base for Therapists

Structure of Week 5

1. Welcome (5 mins)
2. Flash mindfulness (5)
3. The week in review (15)
4. Mindfulness in the therapeutic context (10)
5. Greeting the client (20)
6. Finding your roots (20)
7. Home practice (5)
8. Questions (5)
9. Flash mindfulness (5)

Materials

- Singing bowl
- Timer

1. Welcome

2. Flash mindfulness (Exercise 5, Chapter 3.1)

3. The week in review

4. Mindfulness in the therapeutic context

Begin this session with a short reflection exercise (outlined in Chapter 3.5). Ask participants to reflect for a few moments on each of the following in a gentle, accepting manner:

- How do you feel about being a therapist?
- How do you feel about your work, your colleagues, your clients?
- Can mindfulness help you become more aware of your own needs?
- What impact does this kind of attention have on your health and well-being?
- What influence does it have on your clients and how you work with them?
- How do you find the process of self-reflection?

Don't rush this. Afterwards, ask the group to feed back what they noticed. Use their feedback as the basis for a discussion about the potential of mindfulness to help therapists recognise their own needs (Chapter 3.5).

5. Greeting the client

Ask participants to close their eyes and ask them to imagine how they normally greet their clients (Chapter 3.5). Ask them to imagine themselves in their office or workplace and spend some time reflecting on the first action they take. It could be opening the door, or it might begin even earlier – for example, reading the client's notes from the last session. After this reflection ask them to get into small groups and reflect on their own experiences and to consider how they could do this more mindfully. Then discuss the points raised together as a group.

6. Finding your roots

Lead participants through Exercise 16 (Tree meditation) and Exercise 17 (Stabilising asanas, Chapter 3.5). Afterwards ask for feedback and discuss any issues which emerge.

7. Home practice

- Exercise 5: Flash mindfulness (three times daily).
- Mindfulness diary (daily).
- Exercise 16: Tree meditation and/or Exercise 17: Stabilising asanas (daily).
- Experiment with bringing mindful awareness to the way you greet your clients.
- Check in with yourself during conversations in your private life. How are you? Name thoughts, feelings and sensations (daily).
- Exercise 13: Sitting meditation (daily, minimum 15 minutes).

8. Questions

9. Flash mindfulness to close

Week 6: Mindfulness of the Body

Structure of Week 6

1. Welcome (5 mins)
2. Flash mindfulness (5)
3. The week in review (15)
4. Introducing mindful movement in the office (5)
5. Easing back (10)
6. Shoulder–neck movements (5)
7. Revival (10)
8. Reducing tension and anger (10)
9. Calming/relaxation (10)
10. Home practice (5)
11. Questions (5)
12. Flash mindfulness (5)

Materials

• Timer

1. Welcome

2. Flash mindfulness (Exercise 5, Chapter 3.1)

3. The week in review

4. Introducing mindful movement in the office

You can use any comments participants made about experimenting with Exercise 17 (Stabilising asanas, Chapter 3.5) as the basis for a discussion on mindful movement and mindfulness of the body. You might like to emphasise that mindful movement seems to suit some people better than others and that this session is an invitation to explore mindful movement for themselves. It might also be useful to highlight that the exercises can stand alone or be used sequentially. Emphasise that participants need to be aware of their own limits and are welcome to sit any movement out or adapt it to suit their needs. Also, remind the group that pain is always a sign to stop!

5. Easing back

Lead the participants through Exercise 19 and the variations (Easing back, Chapter 3.6). The variation at the desk may be particularly useful as it can very easily be integrated into participants' working day.

6. Shoulder–neck movements

Guide the group through the sequence of movements presented in Exercise 20 (Shoulder–neck area, Chapter 3.6).

7. Revival

The next sequence is Exercise 21 (Revival, Chapter 3.6). This can be invigorating and is a useful 'pick me up' if participants are feeling tired in the afternoon.

8. Reducing tension and anger

The sequence of movements in Exercise 22 (Reducing tension and anger, Chapter 3.6) may be particularly useful if participants are feeling tense or angry.

9. Calming/relaxation

Exercise 23 (Calming/relaxation, Chapter 3.6) aims to help participants relax. At the end of this sequence ask participants to share their experiences of the mindful movement sequences.

10. Home practice

- Exercise 5: Flash mindfulness (3 times daily).
- Mindfulness diary (daily).
- Practise one of the mindful movement sequences (Exercise 19–23) daily. If you do not want to practise mindful movement, please practise Exercise 13 (daily, minimum 15 minutes).

11. Questions

12. Flash mindfulness (Chapter 3.1)

Week 7: Integrating Mindfulness into Therapeutic Practice

Structure of Week 7

1. Welcome (5 mins)
2. Flash mindfulness (5)
3. The week in review (15)
4. Picture and release (10)
5. Mindful listening (25)
6. Burnout (10–15)
7. Heart meditation (10)
8. Home practice

9. Questions
10. Flash mindfulness

Materials

- Singing bowl
- Timer

1. Welcome

2. Flash mindfulness (Exercise 5, Chapter 3.1)

3. The week in review

4. Picture and release

Discuss some of the challenges of working with draining clients (Chapter 2, Chapter 3.7). You might invite the participants to give some examples of how this makes them feel and how it impacts their lives. Following this, guide the participants through Exercise 24 (Picture and release, Chapter 3.7). Afterwards, you might ask the group how they found the exercise. You could repeat the exercise if appropriate.

5. Mindful listening

Ask the participants to get into pairs and then lead the group through Exercise 25 and the extension of the exercise (outlined in Chapter 3.7). Ask participants how they found it. Use their feedback as the basis of a discussion on how mindful listening can be used in the therapeutic context, drawing out the associated benefits and challenges (Chapter 2, Chapter 3.7).

6. Burnout

Burnout is a key concern for many therapists, so allow plenty of time for this. Based on the material in Chapter 2, discuss the increased risks of therapeutic activity:

- Burnout
- Substance abuse
- Difficulties in their personal relationships
- Empathy fatigue
- Transgressions by clients

Discuss some of the dialectics of therapeutic activity:

- Confidential relationship versus professional role ('rent a friend')
- Professional competence versus personal weakness
- Advances attributed to clients versus failures attributed to the therapist
- Clients feeling better after a session with therapists often feeling drained

Finally, based on participants' reflections and personal experience of mindfulness so far, discuss as a group how mindfulness may help deal with the demands of being a therapist. Mindfulness provides the space to choose how to respond. There are many possible answers, but here are a few examples:

- Focus on current experience versus focus on expectations
- Attention to what is happening versus avoidance or denial
- Non-judgmental acceptance versus ignoring the truth
- Conscious stimulus reduction versus overwhelmed by an experience

7. Heart meditation

Guide the group through Exercise 26 (Chapter 3.7). At the end of the exercise ask participants for feedback and discuss any points raised.

8. Home practice

- Exercise 5: Flash mindfulness (three times daily).
- Mindfulness diary (daily).
- Listen mindfully in personal interactions (daily).
- Exercise 13: Sitting meditation (daily, minimum 15 minutes), followed by Exercise 26: Heart meditation (minimum ten minutes).

9. Questions

10. Flash mindfulness (Chapter 3.1)

Week 8: Review and Next Steps

The eighth session is used to reflect on participants' experience of the programme and discuss how they can move forward, integrating mindfulness into their own personal and professional lives. You might like to cover:

- The key aim of the programme
  - Developing a personal practice
  - Integrating mindfulness into participants' personal and professional lives
- Benefits and challenges

Exercise 27 (walking meditation, Chapter 3.8) is a nice exercise to include in the last session as it can help participants think about how they plan to build mindfulness into their lives. Following on from it, ask the participants to take some time to consider how they wish to incorporate mindfulness practice into their lives (see Chapter 3.8) as they 'move forward'. Ask them to make a few notes about this during the

Table 5.1 Mindful Oasis: A Day of Meditation

Topics		*Time (min)*
1	Welcome	1
2	Flash mindfulness (Exercise 5)	5
3	Group check in	5
4	Structure of the day	5
5	Seated mindfulness (Exercise 4)	20
6	Keeping pace with the breath (Exercise 29)	10
7	Tree meditation (Exercise 16)	15
8	Everyday mindfulness 'tea' (Exercise 12)	15
9	BREAK	10
10	Heart meditation (Exercise 26)	15
11	Yoga (Exercises 19–23)	60
12	LUNCH	60
13	Non-judgmental description of what you see outside (Exercise 8)	20
14	Singing bowl meditation	15
15	Auditory field (Exercise 7)	15
16	Mindful eating (Exercise 28)	15
17	Leaves on a river (Exercise 14)	15
18	BREAK	15
19	Sitting meditation (Exercise 11)	15
20	Walking meditation (Exercise 27)	5
21	Sitting meditation (Exercise 11)	15
22	One-word feedback	5

session. It is very easy to forget to do this and it can help to have something in writing.

Encourage the participants to consider forming or joining a regular meditation circle. Meeting up regularly to practise in a group is very beneficial.

End the session with Exercise 11 (Sitting meditation, Chapter 3.3).

Mindful Oasis

An extended meditation session is a great way to end the programme. We recommend a period of seven hours (including a lunch break). The aim is to spend the majority of the day in silence if possible – including the lunch break.

Because the exercises will all be familiar to the participants, only minimal guidance is necessary. We have prepared an example of how this day could look (Table 5.1). Of course you are free to change the structure and contents as you see fit.

6

Frequently Asked Questions (FAQ)

Most of the points addressed in this section have been outlined in the main body of the book. However, based on our experience of running groups with health professionals, there seem to be a few questions that always pop up. These are addressed below.

1. What is the difference between attention and mindfulness?

Attention is a core aspect of mindfulness, although there is much more to mindfulness than just attention. Mindfulness includes deliberate awareness of the present moment,

Mindfulness for Therapists: Understanding Mindfulness for Professional Effectiveness and Personal Well-Being, First Edition. Gerhard Zarbock, Siobhan Lynch, Axel Ammann and Silka Ringer.
Companion Website: www.wiley.com/go/zarbock/mindfulnessfortherapists

while at the same time accepting what is there without judging it, and letting go of the thoughts and feelings associated with it before returning the attention to the present moment.

2. How important is it to have a regular, formal practice?

If you want to experience the benefits associated with mindfulness in your life (personal or professional), regular practice is essential. You wouldn't expect to see the physical benefits associated with regular workouts if you joined a gym but never attended. It is the same with regular mindfulness practice.

We feel that a regular personal mindfulness practice is absolutely necessary if you use mindfulness in your work with others. As you practise regularly, you gain a deeper appreciation of how the different elements of mindfulness work together – in theory and in your own life. This personal experience is the foundation of introducing mindfulness to others and supporting them as they develop their own practice. Mindfulness sounds very simple when you read about it, but it is only by practising that you gain an appreciation of its subtle nuances.

If you have difficulty making time to practise, it may be worth taking a few moments to reflect on why you want to practise and be honest with yourself about how committed you are. You don't have to commit to it for the rest of your life! If you're finding it difficult, why not try 30 days of regular practice? You can then reappraise things. If 30 days feels too much, how about starting with one or two weeks?

3. I fall asleep when I'm meditating. Is that ok?

Yes and no. If you're falling asleep, then you're probably quite tired already and in need of more rest. So, from that perspective, it is OK. Many people, especially those who are very stressed, overworked or anxious, often say that practising some of the exercises has led them to feel more relaxed than they have in years. Some participants on our courses reported using meditation as a way of getting off to sleep. However, if you regularly fall asleep (or get very sleepy) during your meditation, it is important to be clear that sleeping is not the same as meditation! If you have difficulty sleeping, you might like to try body relaxation exercises to help you get to sleep.

If you are practising lying down, try sitting up. It is often very tempting to practise lying down, especially if you're already tired. Next time you notice yourself deciding to practise lying down, you could use it as a moment of reflection. Why do I want to meditate this way? If you realise you actually need a rest (or even a power nap), why not take one? Just don't forget your meditation practice!

If you find yourself getting sleepy when you're sitting up, notice how you're sitting. Are you slumped in the chair or leaning on the backrest? Why do you choose to sit this way? Are you particularly tired? Would it be helpful to do some mindful movement first? Be honest with yourself. Whether you're sitting on the floor or a chair, try sitting with your back upright and away from the back of the chair (or any other support). Feel free to experiment with your position until you find the right one for you.

It is quite common for a part of the body (foot, leg, arm) to 'go to sleep' during meditation. Some meditation teachers suggest you shouldn't move a part of your body that has gone to sleep but to simply be aware of it instead. We do not share this view. If an area has gone to sleep there may be undue pressure on that area. If you notice that an area has gone to sleep we suggest you try breathing into it in the first instance. If that doesn't help, you could try making a few 'micro-movements', by slightly tensing and relaxing the area. If that doesn't lead to an improvement, we suggest that you move position very carefully. After you finish your practice, always make sure you move a little before you try to stand up!

4. I sometimes feel restless and find myself short of breath when I try to meditate

This is really common. If you experience this, you might like to try the following short exercise at the beginning of your meditation session.

Begin by taking a long, deep breath and holding it for between 10–60 seconds (depending on what is comfortable for you), before breathing out slowly. Take a few normal breaths and then take another long, deep breath, and for about half of the time you took for the first breath (i.e. 5–30 seconds), before breathing out normally. For the next few minutes (3–5) breathe in at a normal pace but breathe out more slowly. After this you should no longer experience the shortness of breath.

5. I'm frustrated because I can't seem to meditate properly. What do you suggest?

When participants on our courses first start to meditate, they often report feeling frustrated because they can't meditate 'properly'. When we ask them what they mean by this they usually say they feel a failure because they can't empty their minds. It is actually very normal for your mind to wander during meditation. In mindfulness meditation, the aim is to become aware of your thoughts and feelings in a gentle and accepting manner. Then, when you're ready, you can choose to let them go. It really doesn't matter how many times your mind wanders when you meditate. In fact, your mind wandering offers you another opportunity to choose to bring your attention back and strengthen your mindfulness practice.

6. I'm interested in further training, what can you recommend?

Our programme is specifically aimed at the needs of therapists and those in the helping professions. If you'd like to explore other mindfulness training programmes, which are secular and follow the eight-week group format, we recommend the following:

- **Mindfulness-Based Stress Reduction (MBSR)**. MBSR was developed by Jon Kabat-Zinn and colleagues to help patients deal with chronic pain and stress and was the first modern Western mindfulness programme.
- **Mindfulness-Based Cognitive Therapy (MBCT)**. MBCT was developed by Mark Williams, Zindel Segal and John Teasdale, to help prevent relapse in patients with depression. It has been widely successful and there are a range of MBCT programmes available.
- **Breathworks Mindfulness for Health**. Breathworks was founded by Vidyamala Burch, who began exploring mindfulness back in 1976 after a severe spinal injury as a teenager. Breathworks Mindfulness for Health programmes

are aimed at individuals with severe and chronic pain. They also offer Mindfulness for Stress programmes and place an emphasis on compassion.

- **Mindfulness-Based Eating Awareness Training (MB-EAT).** MB-EAT was developed by Jean Kristeller and colleagues and focuses on how mindfulness can help individuals become aware of their relationship with food.

There are increasing numbers of other, client-specific training programmes around. We suggest you conduct a thorough internet search.

If you are interested in exploring mindfulness training from a Buddhist perspective, we suggest you approach your local Buddhist centre. Buddhist centres usually provide 'introduction to meditation' classes and host regular meditation circles. If you are interested in mindfulness practice from a Christian perspective, you might like to explore the work of St Ignatius of Loyola.

7. I am interested in mindful movement. What do you suggest?

If you are interested in exploring mindfulness from a movement perspective, you might like to explore the following:

- **Tai Chi or Qi Gong.** While these practices have their roots in Chinese medicine and philosophy, to our knowledge there are not usually any formal prayers in classes, although they usually begin with a bow to the teacher, and the exercises are based on Eastern concepts such as 'yin' or 'yang'.

- **Yoga.** Although yoga is from the Hindu tradition, most yoga classes available in sports centres are ideologically neutral. More traditional forms of yoga are also available.
- **Alexander Technique**. The Alexander Technique was developed by Frederick M. Alexander as a way to help him manage his health problems. The Alexander Technique encourages body-awareness and is popular with actors and musicians. It is usually taught one to one.
- **Feldenkrais**. Feldenkrais was developed by Moshe Feldenkrais and focuses on developing awareness through a variety of subtle movements. It can be taught in groups or one to one.

Further Reading

If you would like to read more about mindfulness:

Hạnh, T. N. (2008). *The miracle of mindfulness: The classic guide to meditation by the world's most revered master*. London: Random House.

Kabat-Zinn, J. (2006). *Coming to our senses: Healing ourselves and the world through mindfulness*. New York: Hyperion.

Kabat-Zinn, J., & Hạnh, T. N. (2009). *Full catastrophe living: Using the wisdom of your body and mind to face stress, pain, and illness*. New York: Random House LLC.

Williams, J. M. G., & Kabat-Zinn, J. (Eds.). (2013). *Mindfulness: Diverse perspectives on its meaning, origins and applications*. London: Routledge.

Mindfulness for Therapists: Understanding Mindfulness for Professional Effectiveness and Personal Well-Being, First Edition. Gerhard Zarbock, Siobhan Lynch, Axel Ammann and Silka Ringer.
© 2015 John Wiley & Sons, Ltd. Published 2015 by John Wiley & Sons, Ltd.
Companion Website: www.wiley.com/go/zarbock/mindfulnessfortherapists

If you would like to focus more on compassion:

Germer, C. K. (2009). *The mindful path to self-compassion: Freeing yourself from destructive thoughts and emotions*. New York: Guilford Press.
Gilbert, P. (2014). *The compassionate mind*. London: Constable & Robinson.
Neff, K. (2011). *Self compassion*. London: Hachette.

If you would like to read more on the neuroscience of mindfulness:

Rizzolatti, G., & Sinigaglia, C. (2008). *Mirrors in the brain: How our minds share actions and emotions*. Oxford: Oxford University Press.
Schmidt, S., & Walach, H. (2013). Meditation–neuroscientific approaches and philosophical implications. *Studies in Neuroscience, Consciousness and Spirituality* (vol. 2). Heidelberg: Springer.
Siegel, D. J. (2007). *The mindful brain: Reflection and attunement in the cultivation of well-being (Norton Series on Interpersonal Neurobiology)*. New York: WW Norton & Company.
Siegel, D. J. (2010). *The mindful therapist: A clinician's guide to mindsight and neural integration*. New York: WW Norton & Company.
Walach, H., Schmidt, S., & Jonas, W. B. (2011). *Neuroscience, consciousness and spirituality* (vol. 1). Heidelberg: Springer.

Finally, we have included some general reading which may be of interest:

Alon, R. (1995). *Mindful spontaneity: Lessons in the Feldenkrais Method*. Berkeley, CA: North Atlantic Books.
Barker, M. (2013). *Mindful counselling and psychotherapy: Practising mindfully across approaches and issues*. London: Sage.
Burch, V., & Penman, D. (2013). *Mindfulness for health (enhanced edition): A practical guide to relieving pain, reducing stress and restoring wellbeing*. London: Piatkus.
Chödrön, P. (2002). *When things fall apart*. Boston, MA: Shambhala Publications.

Further Reading

Hạnh, T. N. (2011). *Anger: Buddhist wisdom for cooling the flames.* London: Random House.

Zajonc, A. (2009). *Meditation as contemplative inquiry: When knowing becomes love.* Great Barrington, MA: Lindisfarne Books.

About the Companion Website

This book is accompanied by a companion website:

www.wiley.com/go/zarbock/mindfulnessfortherapists

About the Companion Website

The website includes the following recordings of meditations:

Chapter	Exercise	Title
3.1	1	What is there?
	2	Breath concentration
	3	Finding your 'relaxed, upright position'
	4	Seated mindfulness
	5	Flash mindfulness
3.2	6	Pre-tree
	7	Auditory field
	8	Non-judgmental description
	9	Short meditation
3.3	10	Energise
	11	Sitting meditation
	12	Everyday mindfulness 'tea'
3.4	13	Sitting meditation (with 'non-responsiveness')
	14	Leaves on a river
	15	In a nutshell
3.5	16	Tree meditation
	17	Stabilising asanas
	18	'There is…'
3.6	19	Easing back
	20	Shoulder–neck area
	21	Revival
	22	Reducing tension and anger
	23	Calming/relaxation
3.7	24	Picture and release
	25	Mindful listening
	26	Heart meditation
3.8	27	Mindful walking
3.9	28	Mindful eating (apple)
	29	Keeping pace with the breath

The material is available free of charge.

Index

Mindfulness for Therapists: Understanding Mindfulness for Professional Effectiveness and Personal Well-Being, First Edition. Gerhard Zarbock, Siobhan Lynch, Axel Amman and Silka Ringer.
© 2015 John Wiley & Sons, Ltd. Published 2015 by John Wiley & Sons, Ltd.
Companion Website: www.wiley.com/go/zarbock/mindfulnessfortherapists

Index